the
facebook
marketing
book

Dan Zarrella and Alison Zarrella

O'REILLY®

Beijing · Cambridge · Farnham · Köln · Sebastopol · Tokyo

The Facebook Marketing Book

by Dan Zarrella and Alison Zarrella

Copyright © 2011 Dan Zarrella and Alison Zarrella. Printed in Canada.

Published by O'Reilly Media, Inc., 1005 Gravenstein Highway North, Sebastopol, CA 95472.

O'Reilly books may be purchased for educational, business, or sales promotional use. Online editions are also available for most titles (*http://my.safaribooksonline.com*). For more information, contact our corporate/institutional sales department: (800) 998-9938 or *corporate@oreilly.com*.

Editor: Julie Steele

Production Editor: Rachel Monaghan

Production Services:
  Newgen North America, Inc.

Copyeditor: Linda Laflamme

Proofreader: Rachel Monaghan

Indexer: Denise Getz

Interior Designer: Ron Bilodeau

Cover Designer: Monica Kamsvaag

Illustrator: Robert Romano

Printing History:
  December 2010: First Edition.

ISBN: 978-1-449-38848-5

[TM]   [2011-04-01]

For my mother, who showed me that you can achieve your dreams if you try hard enough.
I love you, Mom, and you'll be happy to know I've finally realized the value of all those words-of-the-day.

–Dan

For my mom, who recognized my great love of books at a young age and was always ready to listen to my next story. I love you, Mom. (Even though you still haven't figured out how to upload a Facebook photo.)

–Alison

Contents

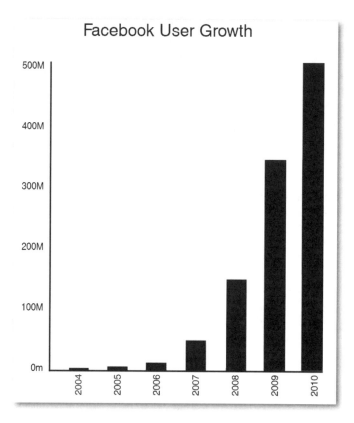

Figure 1-1. The number of active users on Facebook has grown tremendously over the past six years.

CHAPTER 1

Introduction to Social Networking

At the time of this writing, Facebook reports over 500 million active users (Figure 1-1). If it were a country, Facebook would be the third largest nation in the world, lagging behind only China and India. Half of those "citizens" log in every day—that's 250 million people using the site on a daily basis.

Who Uses Facebook?

Originally a network for select college students, Facebook first expanded into high schools, then larger networks, collecting students and colleagues across the country and, eventually, the world. Now you can not only identify your romantic partner and growing circle of friends, but also your parents and siblings. Your mom is on Facebook. Your sister is, and your daughter as well. Your college roommate, your first crush, and the former best friend you haven't spoken to in years. Your grandparents may even be tagging you in family photos you forgot existed. Seventy percent of Facebook users live outside the United States. The fastest growing segment of users? Women 55 to 65 years old. Depending on how you measure it, Facebook either has already surpassed Google in traffic levels or is about to. The Facebook Application platform alone has been used by over one million developers to build more than 500,000 active applications.

Try to pinpoint the "average" user, and you'll find most users are anything but average. Typically, a Facebook user has 130 friends, is connected to 80 Pages, Groups, and Events, and has created 90 pieces of content. Where else could you find someone who talks to over 100 people a day? And that's not even accounting for "super users" or influencers who often have thousands of friends.

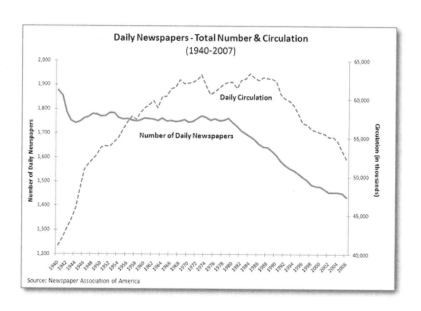

Figure 1-2. The number of daily newspapers published in the US is down, as are their circulation numbers.

Impact on Today's Media

Newspaper circulation rates are in decline (Figure 1-2), and most television ads aren't profitable. Facebook has a far larger audience than old media. That alone has been enough to convince some that it's the perfect place to try a new marketing plan. If you need more incentive, consider the huge amount of personal information that users give the site and, therefore, advertisers. Facebook provides brands with new ways to target ads more effectively than ever before. The best part? All of this information has been *volunteered* by users. In many cases, they have actively opted in to more targeted advertising by "liking" ads or allowing Facebook to share their data with select external sites and partners.

Big Brands on Facebook

The world's largest and most well-known brands are leveraging Facebook to build engaged and profitable communities. Coca-Cola has over 11 million fans of its Page, while Starbucks is closing in on 13 million. Vitamin Water launched an extremely successful contest on Facebook to choose the flavor, design the package, and name its newest drink. The company now has 1.7 million fans.

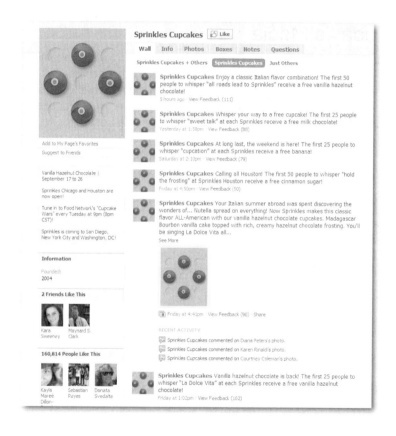

Figure 1-3. Sprinkles Cupcakes is a good example of a small business leveraging Facebook to improve its marketing.

Furniture giant IKEA announced the opening of a new location by posting showroom photos to Facebook. But it didn't stop there. Each item in the photo was up for grabs and given away to the first user to tag a piece with his or her own name. Within hours, thousands of people were scrambling to tag the pictures. Software maker Adobe targeted college students with its Photoshopped or Not game, asking users to decide whether an image had been manipulated. Six percent of students who saw the game clicked on a Buy Now button. To promote the launch of a vampire movie, Sony rebranded its popular Vampires application and launched a sweepstakes. In three weeks, it drew more than 59,000 entries.

How You Can (and Should) Use Facebook

Even small brands can get in on the action. Sprinkles Cupcakes (Figure 1-3) has more than 150,000 fans because of a Facebook-only promotion that ran in its stores. Luxury hotel chain Joie De Vivre offered a similar Facebook-only discount and booked more than 1,000 rooms because of the deals. Your existing and potential customers and all of their friends and family are not only on Facebook, but also logging in regularly and engaging with content on the site. Your competitors are probably already there, too. If you're not on Facebook, you need to play catch-up to avoid appearing out of touch. If your competitors are not yet using Facebook, you'll gain major points with your audience by being there first.

Figure 1-4. Even Facebook itself has a Facebook Page.

Creating Valuable Content

If used properly, Facebook can be an extension of your brand, helping you present the same personality, tone, and visual face as you would in any other material. Take the time to think about why you and your brand want to engage Facebook and what you hope to achieve from doing so. But don't stop there. Think about your audience, specifically the segment of your audience on Facebook.

Facebook is a highly competitive and fast-moving channel. Each piece of content you post needs to be quickly digestible and easily recognizable in a busy newsfeed. Above all else, it needs to fit the unofficial model of a Facebook post. Do not copy and paste from your website or email campaign. Each post should be specific to your Facebook Page. Keep it short and to the point. Add media to spice things up, and make it clear what action you want users to take.

Facebook marketing can be amazingly cost effective, especially when compared to traditional media alternatives, but expect to make a significant time investment. Facebook users expect you to listen to their demands (and actually act on them, not just say "we hear you"). They want interesting and regularly updated content, and they want exclusive offers for being your "friend."

Facebook offers a variety of tools and platforms to reach users. Marketers can leverage Facebook Ads, applications, Pages, or Events. Each of these tools also contains an analytics system called Insights that easily reports on activity levels and demographics (Figure 1-4). This book will walk you through all of these and more to help you create effective and profitable campaigns.

CHAPTER 2

Facebook Profile Basics

A *Profile* is a digital representation of a Facebook user's self. Profiles are a thing of pride for frequent Facebook users—an extension of their personalities. Profiles are how users share things with their large and very connected group of social connections. For marketers, the Profile is where it all begins.

To reach and engage these socially connected influencers, you must know what they do and enjoy on the site. Remember, the most valuable Facebook users are the ones who provide a lot of information and have vast connections. The average user has 130 friends; think about the potential of these super-users. Their Profile upkeep requires time and energy to stay fresh, personal, and relevant to friends (and, of course, to marketers like you).

In total, users spend over 70 billion minutes on Facebook per month. You need to appreciate the dedication and openness it takes to create a complete Facebook Profile, because the owners of these Profiles will be the ones that spend a few of those precious minutes helping you gain buzz, clicks, or sales. The best way to understand and appreciate these Facebook users and their Profiles is to create your own.

Figure 2-1. You can view a variety of information on an active Facebook user's Profile.

What Is a Facebook Profile?

A Facebook Profile is the way individual users represent themselves on the site (Figure 2-1). Typically it contains information about the user's interests, hobbies, school and work affiliations, and photos. It is also connected to any Facebook Pages he likes, from a favorite football team to a preferred brand of soda, as well as all the other Facebook users he identifies as friends.

Many users are quite open with their Profile information, and Facebook strongly encourages this. Because the site is free, Facebook's big moneymaking opportunity comes from charging marketers for the right to use the personal data its users share; the more data users freely provide, the more potential revenue for the site. Some users have expressed concern over privacy issues, particularly regarding Facebook's increasingly open view of "public" information on their site. Expanded privacy settings have allowed many users to customize their information as "for friends only," but most users, especially younger generations, are happy to share every detail of their lives. They understand and appreciate that this means a more personalized site experience and enjoy connecting with the brands they know and love.

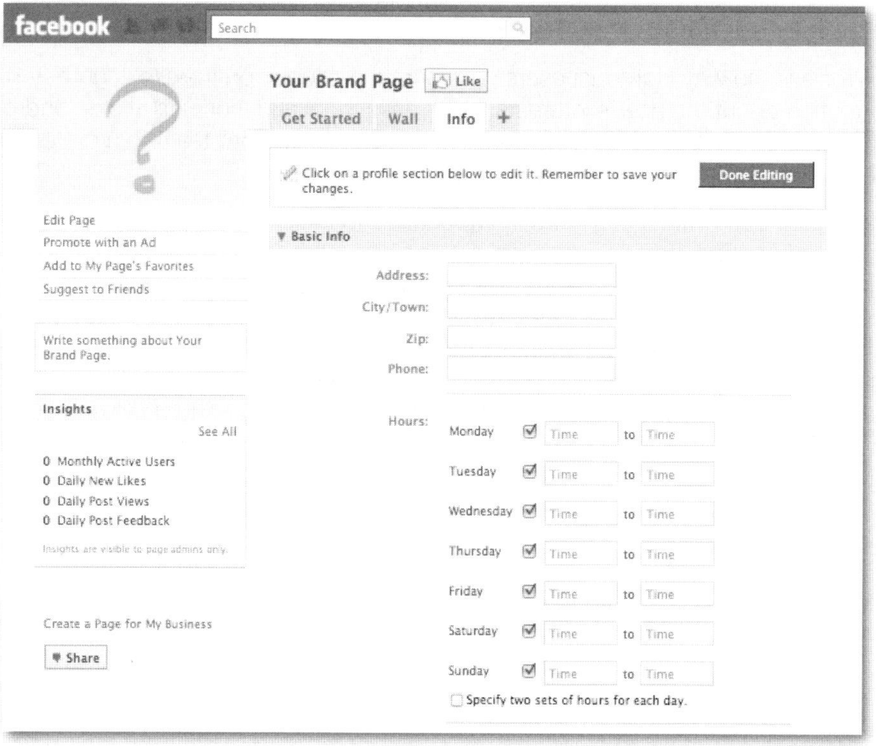

Figure 2-2. The beginnings of a basic Facebook Profile. You will need one in order to manage a Facebook Page for marketing purposes.

Facebook Profiles for Business

Facebook's original intention was to be a social network for college students, and at one time it required an .edu email address for registration. Later, it expanded to grant membership to high school students, and finally to people of all ages. However, keeping true to its origins as a service geared to connecting individuals, Facebook has always maintained certain rules for brands and businesses.

One rule many marketers find frustrating is Facebook's strong distinction between the types of users and how it applies that distinction to Profiles. If you represent a brand or entity other than an individual user, Facebook's Terms of Service state that you must set up a Facebook Page to represent that brand, business, or public persona, whatever it may be. This includes politicians, sports figures, and other celebrities; even as individuals, they need a Page for their very recognizable self. These Pages offer different choices that are specific to companies, such as business hours, and leave out more personal details, such as hobbies and interests.

Still, Facebook Profiles are the building blocks of the site itself, and you'll need to set one up before you can do anything else on the site, including creating a Page of any kind (Figure 2-2). Profiles, and the people they represent, are linked back to every action on Facebook so that someone can be held accountable for each interaction and piece of content that appears on the site.

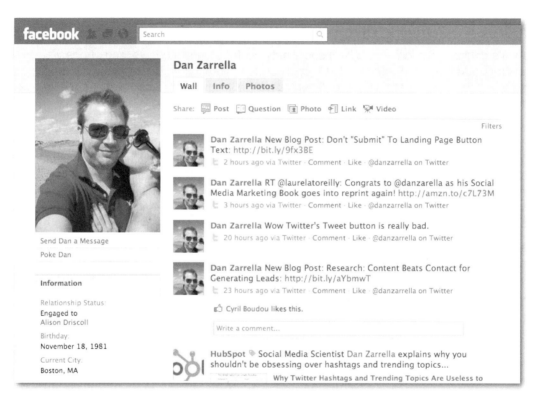

Figure 2-3. A basic Facebook profile has three tabs: Wall, Info, and Photos. More active users may add other custom tabs or applications.

Facebook Profile Tabs

A Facebook Profile has three main tabs: Wall, Info, and Photos (Figure 2-3). Other applications (or *apps*) can add more, but these are the basics that every Profile starts with.

Wall

The Wall tab is the standard landing Page for your Facebook Profile. This is where people can post public messages to you or comment on posts (much like a blog). You can update your status from this tab and view older status updates. Any applications you have authorized to post to your Wall will also appear here, such as an RSS feed or tweets from Twitter.

Info

The Info tab is where all of your personal information—likes, interests, workplace, hometown, email address, and so on—is displayed. Unlike the Wall, there is not much opportunity for interaction between users here. While this tab is arguably the most beneficial and rich in information for Facebook marketers, it is probably the least interesting to the average user.

Photos

The Photos tab has long been a Facebook staple. This tab houses every photo you have uploaded *or* been tagged in. Each tag creates a link back to that user's Profile. Note that only people, and therefore Profiles, can be tagged in a photo, not brands or Pages.

Figure 2-4. The basic information section of a Facebook Profile is full of personal details about the user.

Setting Up a Facebook Profile

Besides the fact that you need at least a bare-bones Profile to set up any marketing efforts on Facebook, you can also use your Profile as a sort of sandbox for trying out different Facebook applications and features. Creating your own Profile will help you understand Profiles from a user perspective. You need to know what users see, do, like, and dislike on the site in order to know what works (and what doesn't) in the world of Facebook marketing.

Basic Information

A user must provide a name, birth date, and email address to sign up for the site; almost every other piece of information is optional or can be hidden. Profile basics include the information that requires very little thought to fill out: gender, birth date, hometown, and the like. Although compulsory, the birthday and gender fields may be hidden from public viewing.

Bio and Quotations

The next section of a Facebook Profile (Figure 2-4) requires a bit more thought. Users have adapted the Bio and Favorite Quotations sections for various purposes. Some users take a straightforward approach, giving a few brief sentences about themselves followed by song lyrics or movie quotes. Others use that space for inside jokes, while yet another group treats it as space for a résumé.

How someone chooses to fill in these open-ended boxes reveals a lot: language, grammar, and depth of information tell a story outside of the words themselves. Generally, the more a user shares, the more active she is on the site. This makes active, openly sharing users good potential brand ambassadors.

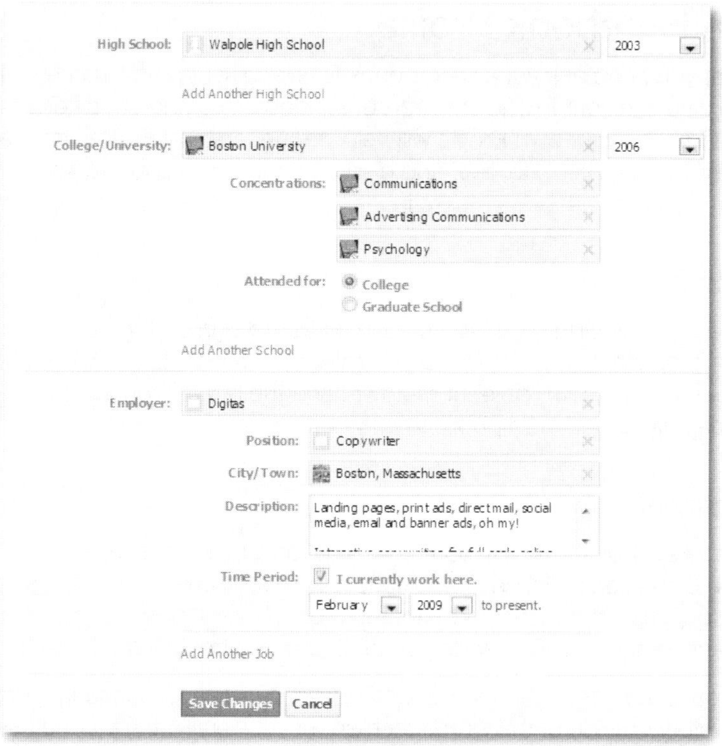

Figure 2-5. *The Work and Education section can be used to create networks and provide clues about a user's potential interests.*

Work and Education

As Facebook shifted its focus from exclusively college students to its current, much more diverse user base, the Work and Education section expanded to accommodate these changes.

Predictive-type drop-down menus allow users to input as many schools as required, going all the way back to high school, and to specify areas of concentration at universities or colleges (Figure 2-5). Facebook uses this information to search for relevant alumni Pages within the site.

Users can also input work experience in much the same way, adding jobs in reverse chronological order as Facebook attempts to match the companies they have worked for with existing Pages. These fields are all some form of drop-down menu, with the exception of the Description box, in which users can enter highlights of what the job entailed or the company's purpose.

While job and education history may be of little interest to many retail brands, this section can be especially helpful if you plan to use Facebook for recruiting purposes. As more and more people turn to Facebook as a way to find new employees, this section may see an increase in emphasis and functionality.

Likes and Interests

Activities	Being a Geek, Blogging
Interests	Red Sox, Bahston, Gym Rat, Lifetime Movies, Thai food, Girlie Movies That Make Me Cry, Fake Sushi, Gamma Phi Beta Sorority, Shopping When I Should Be Saving, Diet Cherry Coke, Advertising, Facebook stalking, Twitter
Music	Dave Matthews, Stephen Kellogg, Fiona Apple, John Mayer, Matt Nathanson, Justin Timberlake, O.A.R., Carbon Leaf, Pink, Kings Of Leon, 311, Kid Rock, Build A Machine, Phoenix, Britney Spears **Show all (25)**
Books	Gone with the Wind, Catcher In The Rye, Thank You for Smoking, A Separate Peace, The Pact, The Notebook, The Wedding, In Her Shoes, Best Friends, Bitter Is the New Black, Bright Lights Big Ass, PS, I Love You, The Starter Wife, Perfect Match, The Bitch Posse **Show all (17)**
Movies	Breakfast at Tiffany's, Legally Blonde 2: Red, White & Blonde, Cruel Intentions, Love Actually, American Beauty, Good Will Hunting, Say Anything..., Office Space, Rebel Without a Cause, Garden State, How to Lose a Guy in 10 Days, Wedding Crashers, The Notebook, 21 Grams, Prime **Show all (19)**
Television	Grey's Anatomy, Tell Me You Love Me, CSI, The Starter Wife, The Mentalist, Sex and the City 2, Entourage, Private Practice, Lipstick Jungle, True Blood, Sex and the City, Jersey Shore, CSI: Crime Scene Investigation, Saved By The Bell, Trust Me **Show all (17)**

Show other Pages

Figure 2-6. Likes and interests are now displayed as links to related Facebook Pages, connecting personal Profiles to brands.

Likes and Interests

According to Facebook, a user's likes and interests include activities, interests, music, books, movies, and television shows. The ease of adding such types of interests through the Like button often makes Likes and Interests the most robust section of a user's Profile (Figure 2-6). In the past, users were able to enter their likes and dislikes in a free-form manner via a text box. As part of Facebook's recent push to connect Profiles to Pages, users now indicate their preferences via the Like button and lists of Page links; simply clicking the Like button on a Page creates a link on the user's Profile. Each Page then describes that interest, as well as a list of users who share that favorite film, show, or other interest. The jury is still out on whether this shift to maximum connectivity helps or hurts Facebook, the average user, or Page administrators and marketers.

Pages

The connectivity shift, however, did impact other aspects of a Profile for Page administrators. Pages that were once displayed quite prominently on a user's Profile are now hidden behind a Show Other Pages link. Back when users still "fanned" a Page, those Pages enjoyed the honor of being the only section of a Profile to contain images. Now that the interests section is linked to Pages, Pages that are liked but not added to the interests section have been pushed back.

Facebook reasons that asking users to "like" a Page, as opposed to "fan" it, requires less of a connection to the Page's subject matter and increases interaction with the site. Yet while users may end up liking more Pages with the new terminology, for a Page to receive prominence on a Profile requires a higher level of dedication than ever before. Sure, you can click to show other Pages, but to have a Page displayed front and center requires a committed assertion; a user must edit her Profile, type an interest, and then connect to a Page.

Figure 2-7. *Most users are open with all their information except contact info. Don't use Facebook as a way to gain email addresses; keep your marketing on Facebook, where you know your target audience is.*

Contact Information

Last, and probably least for most marketers, is the contact information section (Figure 2-7). Some users may find this section helpful for searching and connecting with old friends or taking Facebook communications to a more private venue, but as a marketer on Facebook, you should keep your communications on the site. Still, it's useful to know how the entire Profile section works, and what you can add to yours depending on how accessible you want to be to your audience.

First up is your email address, which is required to register for the site. Users can also add an IM screen name, mobile and land-line phone numbers, a physical mailing address, and a dorm residence, as well as links to additional personal websites that friends might want to visit—such as a blog, Twitter account, or LinkedIn Profile. With the exception of your email address, no field is required. The amount of information visible to the public differs from person to person, but again, generally speaking, younger users seem happy to share IM names and phone numbers, while older members do not.

The privacy controls for this section are more finely tuned than most. Users can control who sees each individual piece of information; settings range from Everyone (the most public option) to Custom settings that allow users to specify only a few friends or members of a certain Friend List. For example, you could decide that everyone can view your email address, but only college and work friends can see your physical address, and just a select few work friends have access to your IM screen name. These privacy adjustments make it possible to fill out your Profile completely and then tailor its appearance to individuals or groups of friends.

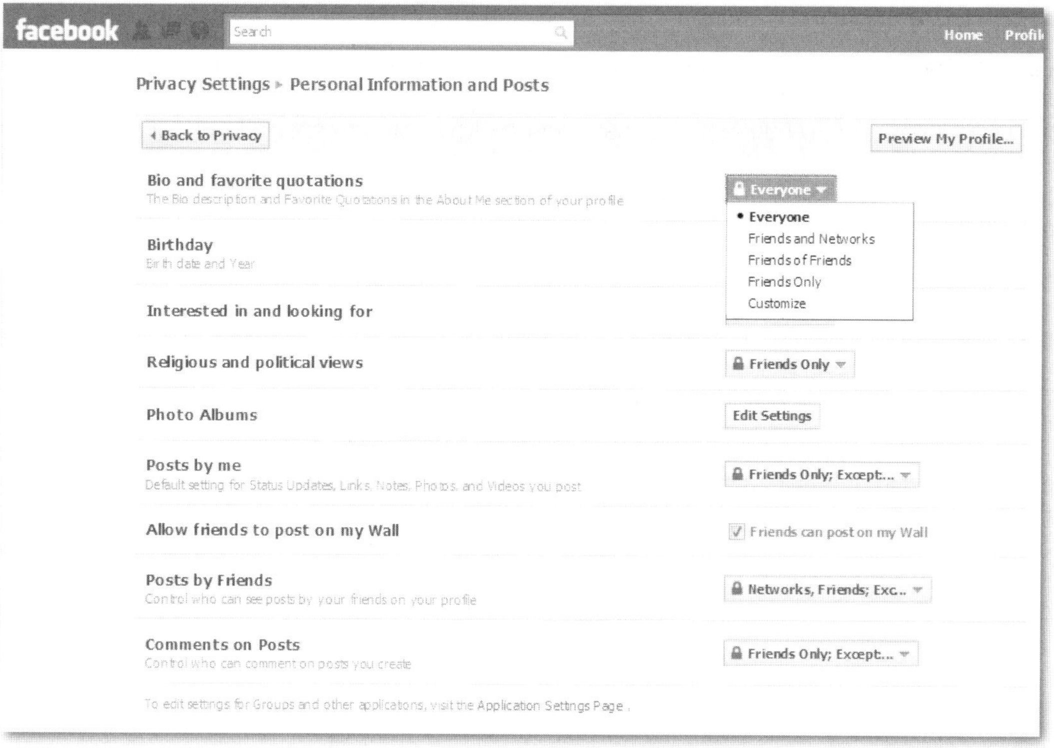

Figure 2-8. Privacy settings are used to show more information to close friends and less to the Internet at large.

Privacy Settings

Along with the ability to add and share all this information online, Facebook also created ways to keep some sections of a Profile more private than others. Some people put up barriers that reflect real life, only accepting friends they personally know. The easiest way to share what you want with whom you want, however, is to use Facebook's built-in privacy settings and friend lists.

As discussed in the previous section, privacy settings (Figure 2-8) allow you to control who can see your contact information. They also allow you to control who can see your personal information, including your birthday, favorite quotes, interests, education and work info, and relationship status. You can also determine who is allowed to post on your wall, tag you in photos or videos, or view your Profile in both Facebook and public search results. Photo album settings are determined on a case-by-case basis, so you can make some albums available to all friends, and others just a select group of people. You can also control what you share with outside websites, as well as what your friends can share about you.

Privacy settings also allow you to see which applications are running on your Profile, adjust app settings, and block or remove old apps you no longer use or want. For marketers, the more open a person keeps his privacy settings, the more data you can collect or use for targeting.

Figure 2-9. Segmenting friends into lists or groups helps users stay organized and adjust privacy settings more efficiently.

Friend lists and groups

To make adjusting privacy settings easier, you can segment your friends into handy groups or lists (Figure 2-9) and fine-tune your settings in bulk. For example, you might create a list for work colleagues and allow them full access to your personal information, but restrict some photo albums. Just keep in mind that a friend's settings are determined by the most restrictive list they belong to. So, if you have a close friend whom you also work with, and you want him to view the most open settings for your Profile, you won't want to lump him in with other work colleagues.

You can also create exceptions to settings to keep only a few people (a former boyfriend or girlfriend, perhaps) from seeing certain parts of your Profile. Just choose Customize from the Privacy Settings menu and select the items you want to hide from certain friends. Then type the friend's name and click Save Settings to keep that piece of information private. Or, if you really don't want to be bothered by someone or to let a person find you at all, you can add her to your block list. Simply scroll to the bottom of her Profile's left navigation column and click Report/Block.

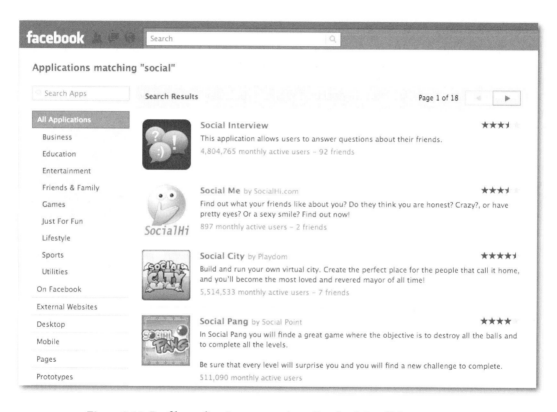

Figure 2-10. Profile applications customize a Facebook Profile's appearance. Creating an application can be a great way to market your brand or company.

Profile Applications

Facebook offers a myriad of applications. These can be useful for marketers, because they provide a naturally viral vehicle for spreading awareness of your brand. Some apps are designed by Facebook and have a more practical utility, such as Photos or Notes. Others are more about fun, like Coke Zero's Facial Profile doppleganger app or Zynga's FarmVille. Anyone can create a Facebook app, which means there are a lot of fun and useful applications available; however, this also means that there are plenty of abandoned apps that never worked quite right.

Most apps are perfectly safe to add to your Profile or Page. However, you should do a little research before adding apps from lesser-known developers. Check out star ratings and user discussions in the Application Directory (Figure 2-10) to make sure the developer is still maintaining the application. You can also see how many active users an app has, as well as what's new or popular across the site.

Once you've found an application you like, click to add it to your Profile or Page, depending on the use and type of app. Some are strictly for Profile use, such as games, while more practical apps, like the custom tab developer Static FBML, can be used for Pages as well.

As Facebook phases out the Boxes tab of Profiles and Pages, applications appear either on their own tab, like the Static FBML custom tab, or as a function of a Profile, like Twitter's status updater. Facebook maintains tight control over how and where items are displayed, and some apps are further restricted by their developers for optimum viewing.

Figure 2-11. A user's Wall includes interactions with friends on the site (other Profiles), brands they like (Pages), posts to the Newsfeed (status updates), and applications usage.

Profile Interactions

There are many ways that a user can interact with your brand on Facebook, from a Page to a custom-branded Application or ad. However, user-to-user interaction is actually a little more limited, despite the categorization of Facebook as a social network.

Facebook friendships are two-way connections; that is, a user must request to *friend* another user and wait for approval before they can talk or interact in any meaningful way. Once that connection has been established, users can use Facebook Chat as well as Facebook's private messaging system (which works much like email). However, the favorite means of communication for frequent Facebook users is *Wall posting* (Figure 2-11).

Facebook is a site founded on connections but is increasingly moving toward more open channels of communication. Heavy Facebook users feed into this change by making many chats completely public. Wall-to-Wall postings often read like email or IM exchanges, and the comments for status updates, link posts, or photo uploads often run well past a simple note. In addition, the more people post or comment, the more other people join in; they want to see what and why everyone is commenting on a particular photo or article and join in the fun.

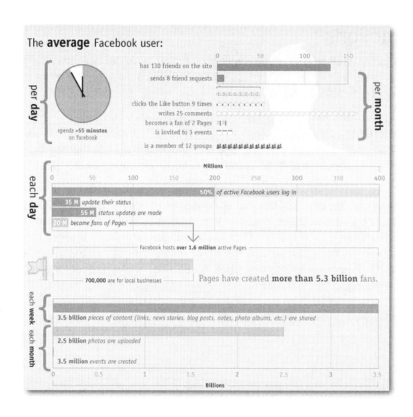

Figure 2-12. Consider a snapshot of the average Facebook user. (Infographic by Muhammad Saleem for Mashable.com.)

Summary

As you can tell, a lot goes into a Facebook Profile. What information you show and how much time you spend updating and maintaining it is up to you and will largely depend on your goals for and use of the Profile. But the Profile is where it all begins and is a major part of every user's Facebook experience, so it's vital that you thoroughly understand how Profiles work, look, and relate to one another.

No matter what kind of brand, product, or service you are marketing, you need a firm understanding of your target. On Facebook, this means getting back to basics and working from the beginning: the Facebook Profile.

According to Facebook, there are currently over 500 million active users on the site, at least half of whom log in every day (Figure 2-12). That means 500 million Profiles that you can use to get data about your target audience. In fact, this is Facebook's biggest selling point: the site actively (some say aggressively) encourages users to fill their Profiles with the type of information marketers are always trying to find—all for free.

CHAPTER 3

Facebook Page Basics

A Facebook Page is key to most social media marketing strategies and will more than likely be the central point for most of your efforts and promotions. Twitter is great for quick updates, but to get the full story, users usually need to click elsewhere. A Facebook Page allows you to provide both in one place, while also offering full customization and a variety of interactions.

Many brands use Facebook tabs in lieu of landing pages on their actual websites, because tabs have more built-in social functionality, are easy to update, and are especially helpful for running contests and promotions. But even if you foresee offering giveaways through tabs, you should still invest some serious setup time in Page customization.

Build your Page for success the first time around by populating it with lots of optimized content and developing a content strategy to keep it fresh. You can spend as much or as little time as you can afford updating and maintaining the Page, and your time input will vary as your goals and use of the Page fluctuate. If you fill out the Page completely and make it interesting and engaging early on, however, it's easier to take some time off later.

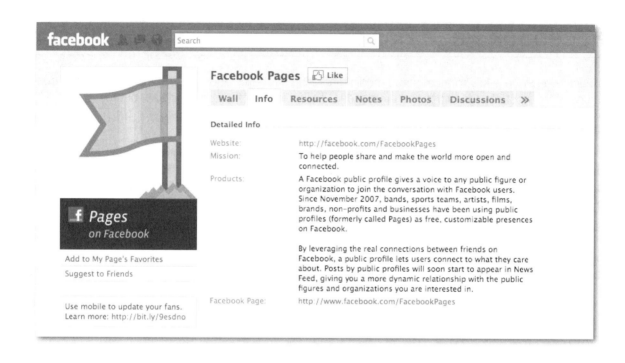

Figure 3-1. Facebook's official Page about Facebook Pages provides helpful hints and tips for Page administrators.

As you read in Chapter 2, Facebook outlines strict rules about who can have a Facebook Profile. In its early years, Facebook was a closed site, accessible only to college students; every user was an individual person and had a unique Profile. When the site opened up to the public, brands were quick to see the potential for reaching people in a new way. At that time, Facebook wasn't anticipating heavy brand participation; the Facebook Ads platform was the only real nod to marketing on the site. So marketers turned to the only option available at the time: personal Profiles.

This worked for a while, as small, local brands could fly under the radar. But the upkeep of a personal Profile for a nonhuman entity is awkward; the questions are a bit far removed from anything except a mascot or spokesperson. What would be the Nike swoosh's favorite movie?

As Facebook started to take notice of brands masquerading as people, it created a place on the site for them (Figure 3-1), instead of kicking them off for abusing the Terms of Service. These terms state that:

- You will not provide any false personal information on Facebook or create an account for anyone other than yourself without permission.

- You will not create more than one personal Profile.

Before the site introduced Pages, Facebook's Terms of Service also specified that only real people could maintain a Profile; technically, creating a Profile for your dog was also against the rules.

Figure 3-2. Notice the variety of brands, public figures, and interests in the top 10 Facebook Pages by fans. (Graphic by www.website-monitoring.com.*)*

The Difference Between a Page and a Profile

The easiest way to determine what warrants a Page versus a Profile is to compare the verbs Facebook uses to interact on the site: *friend* versus *like* (previously *fan*). You *friend* the people you work with, went to school with, or met at a party. You can't actually friend your favorite TV show, college mascot, or flavor of soda. But you can absolutely *like* these things; that is what you would say in real life, and the action you take on the site. The top Facebook Pages (Figure 3-2) exemplify the types of things that you would like, not friend.

That college mascot raises an interesting question. You can't really friend the chicken that danced at football games (although you could friend the guy inside the costume); however, a mascot might have a distinct personality, with favorite quotes, books, and movies, just like the questions asked by a personal Profile. And of course movie stars, authors, and politicians have all the same favorites as the guy sitting next to you on the bus, yet they require a Page as well—at least for their public persona.

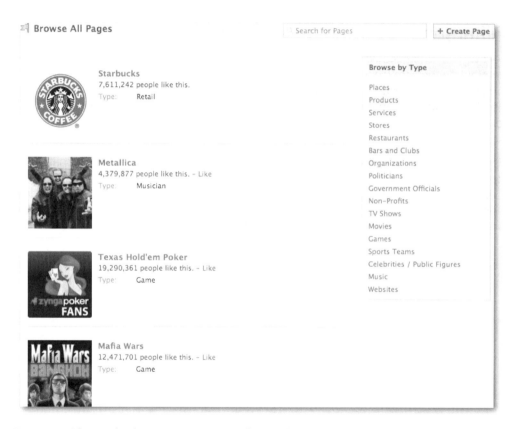

Figure 3-3. The Facebook Page Directory provides another look at some of the top Facebook Pages.

Here again, taking a hard look at the verb use on the site will help. You're not going to actually become friends with the president. Sure, he has friends and may keep a private Profile for real-life friends, but the greater public can only *like* him on Facebook. Public figures, such as musicians, actors, politicians, sports stars, and other people with famous names or faces need to create a Page for public consumption, even though they are, of course, individuals who could also have a personal Profile.

The bottom line? If you're thinking about doing any type of marketing on Facebook, you need to create a Page. As the Facebook Page Directory (Figure 3-3) shows, all types of brands are doing it.

What Requires a Facebook Page, Not a Profile

Still confused between who needs a Profile and what gets a Page? Table 3-1 offers a simple categorization of the types of Pages and their uses.

Brands	Services	People	Stuff
Sports teams	Services	Politicians	Music
Products	Stores	Government officials	Places
Nonprofits	Restaurants	Celebrities/ public figures	TV shows
Websites	Bars and clubs		Movies
	Organizations		Games

Table 3-1. A simpler way to think about the many types and categories of Facebook Pages.

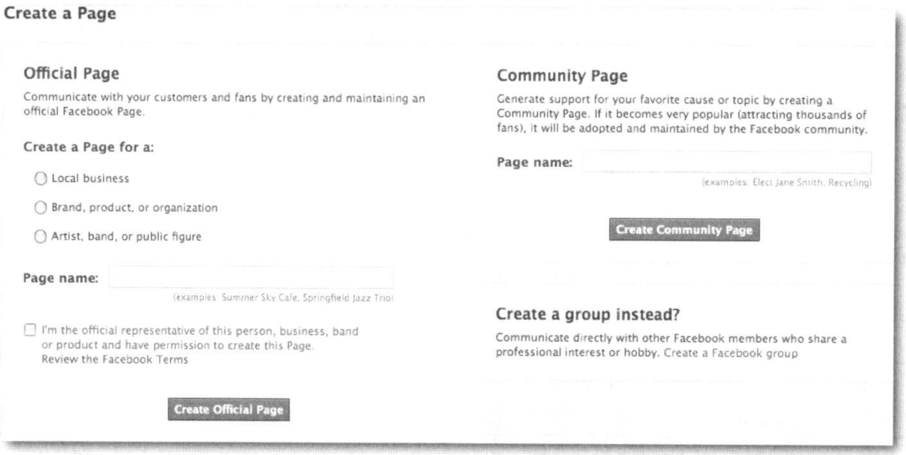

Create a Page

Official Page

Communicate with your customers and fans by creating and maintaining an official Facebook Page.

Create a Page for a:

○ Local business

○ Brand, product, or organization

○ Artist, band, or public figure

Page name: [   ]

(examples: Summer Sky Cafe, Springfield Jazz Trio)

☐ I'm the official representative of this person, business, band or product and have permission to create this Page.
Review the Facebook Terms

[Create Official Page]

Community Page

Generate support for your favorite cause or topic by creating a Community Page. If it becomes very popular (attracting thousands of fans), it will be adopted and maintained by the Facebook community.

Page name: [   ]

(examples: Elect Jane Smith, Recycling)

[Create Community Page]

Create a group instead?

Communicate directly with other Facebook members who share a professional interest or hobby. Create a Facebook group

Figure 3-4. This first step to creating a Facebook Page is found at http://www.facebook.com/advertising/?pages.

Types of Pages

Facebook separates Pages into 17 categories and many subcategories, of which the four most common are:

- Brands
- Services
- People
- Stuff

The Facebook Page setup process (Figure 3-4) will guide you through choosing the right one for your needs.

It's best not to get too hung up on the label you choose for the Page; few people will ever see it anyway. It is displayed next to your name and the number of connections on the search Page, but generally users will already know what you do and are simply trying to find your Page. Once they click Like for your Page, your chosen category is of little or no consequence to them.

Your choice of category *does* matter to the setup and display of your information, however. Different categories ask different types of questions and display different amounts of information. Click around and try a few categories during setup; you can't change your category or Page name once you have created the Page, so take some time in the beginning to make sure the category and information display are what you want.

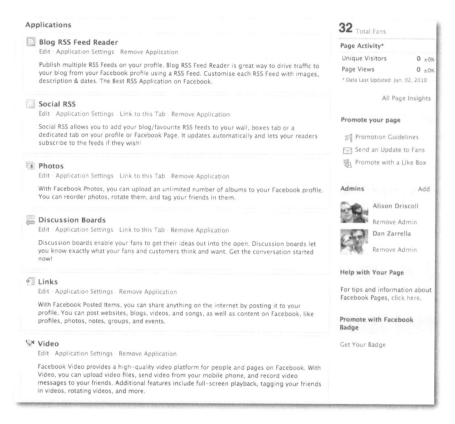

Figure 3-5. *The back end of a Facebook Page shows all the applications used to customize and display content.*

Creating and Customizing a Facebook Page

Once you've chosen a Page name and category, it's time to begin customizing your Page and pulling in or creating content. You don't need to publish your Page right away, so you can keep it hidden while you play around with designs and applications.

Because there are so many options for customization, from Facebook apps to custom applications that you can design yourself (Figure 3-5), it's helpful to create a wireframe or basic design of your Page layout before you begin. You should also develop a content strategy and posting schedule that includes automated feeds from external sites, like an RSS feed from your blog or Twitter page, as well as manual updates and responses you post to the Page in real time.

By searching the Application Directory on Facebook, you can find many free applications with which to begin customizing your Facebook Page. The official Facebook Page about Pages (found at *http://www. facebook.com/FacebookPages*) also offers many tips and resources for Facebook Page administrators, who are more commonly called *admins*.

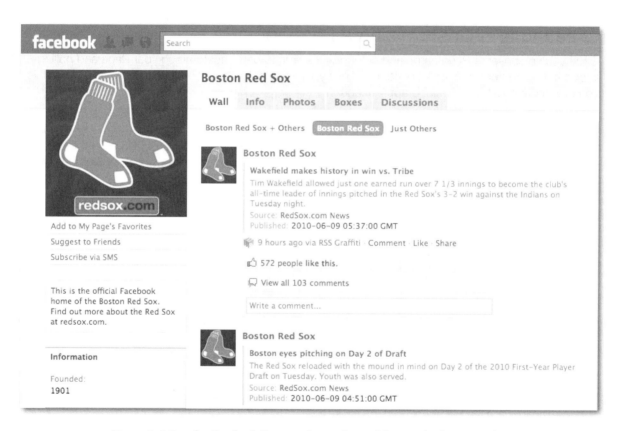

Figure 3-6. Popular Facebook Pages make good use of the standard, preset tabs.

Static FBML, Notes, and Social RSS are three great, free apps to get you started. With these you can quickly customize the look of your Page and start bringing in outside content and adding to your Page's tab structure (Figure 3-6). Keep in mind, though, that a long-term Facebook Page strategy usually benefits from a custom application or more extensive customization with Facebook Markup Language (FBML).

Static FBML

Use Static FBML to create custom boxes or tabs using FBML (similar to HTML). Although doing so requires some coding ability, it's worth the effort. This application will allow you to design a custom landing tab that tells users what you offer and why they should like the Page.

Notes

An official Facebook application, Notes allows you to pull in a blog feed and automatically post to your Wall. This helps you keep a steady stream of content from your website without always having to log in to Facebook. You can also post a manual note, which provides more formatting capabilities than a standard status update.

Social RSS

Social RSS is another good RSS feed app that you can use to create a full tab display of your blog or Twitter feed. If you are a frequent blogger, this app (or one like it) is a necessity. Social RSS enables you to display your blog in its own tab just as it looks on your site, as opposed to displaying a snippet on your Wall.

Figure 3-7. Here's a slightly more complex usage of Facebook Page tabs.

Facebook Page Tabs

Much like a Facebook Profile, a Page has three main tabs: Wall, Info, and Photos. Using an application such as FBML, you can create and add custom tabs as well (Figure 3-7).

Wall

The Wall tab is the standard landing page for your Facebook Page. This is where people can post public messages to you or comment on posts, just like for a blog. You can update your status from this tab and view older status updates. Any applications you have authorized to post to your Wall, such as RSS feeds, will also appear here. Page members can like or comment on any of the posts on your Wall as well.

Info

The Info tab displays all of your company or brand information, such as a mission statement or website. The information available on this tab is dependent upon the category you have chosen for your Page. This tab can also help you increase your presence in Facebook searches, so be thorough.

Photos

The Photos tab has long been a Facebook staple, but it can be a stumbling block for Page admins. For some brands, it is hard to come up with images that people will want to view on Facebook. Product shots don't work on this site; you need to make people want to click through albums. There is a lot to look at on Facebook, so get creative with ways to use your product or have fun with your brand.

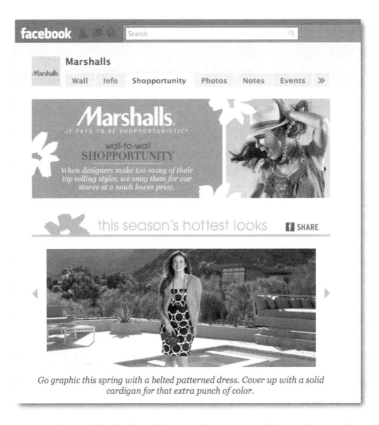

Figure 3-8. This Facebook tab makes use of FBML to add more design elements.

Page Applications

A Facebook Page usually comes preloaded with several Facebook-developed applications, including Photos, Links, Notes, Discussions, Videos, and Events. Many of these existed on the site even before the introduction of Pages or applications, and so it is easy to forget that they are, in fact, Facebook-developed apps.

The functionality of these apps is pretty self-explanatory: each allows you to upload or post the content they are named for. Thus, they provide the basic structure of a Page and the Page members' interactions with content. Your Facebook Page marketing strategy should go far beyond these basic applications, however.

Custom Applications

Facebook allows developers to create all kinds of custom apps. Depending on your size, budget, and strategy, you might want to develop your own custom applications for Page member use or simply to take full control of tab customization and design (Figure 3-8). Readily available, free applications can help you get up and running quickly or add more content, but they provide little control. If something breaks, you must wait for the developer to fix it, and you usually have very little say in how content is displayed on your Page tabs. Using FBML is one option, but for landing tabs or promotions, it is best to design your own applications.

Figure 3-9. Fashion brand Diane von Furstenberg features a robust, interactive custom tab on its Page.

Custom User Applications

Some applications are designed for user interaction and may be only tangentially related to your brand. For example, Coke Zero's Facial Profiler doppelganger app allowed users to find their online twins. Based on the idea that Coke Zero tastes the same as regular Coke, this popular app was fun but didn't really connect the application to the brand. What it did do was allow Coke to advertise to a captive audience.

Zappos, on the other hand, created an application that allows users to share their favorite products from the online retailer with their Facebook friends. Marshalls uses a custom application to ask Page members to unlock their "shopportunity" for a chance to win a shopping spree, while TripAdvisor allows users to display all the cities they have visited. Fashion, technology, and travel play well on Facebook as applications, but get creative and you can create an application that is both fun and relevant in any industry.

Custom Tab Applications

With a custom application, you can create tabs that not only display content any way you want, but also include such interactive elements as polls and quizzes, video players, games, and email capture forms (Figure 3-9). A custom app like this is ideal when designing a landing tab for a Facebook promotion. Although you can also use Static FBML to create custom tabs, it does not provide the full level of customization that an application built to your specifications can offer.

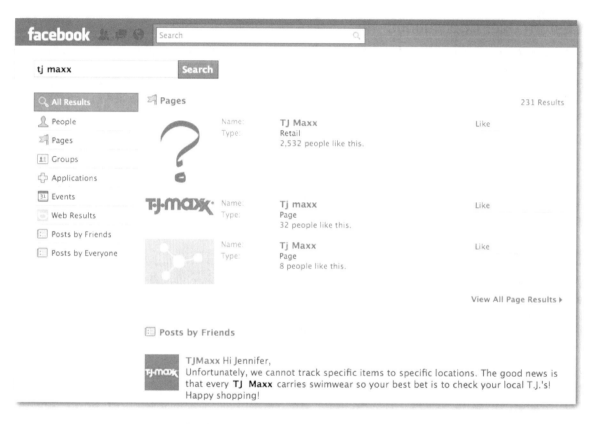

Figure 3-10. An example of poor internal Facebook search results for the T.J. Maxx brand.

Page Optimization

To maximize your *return on investment* (ROI) on Facebook, you want to make sure you are getting and keeping Page members (formerly called fans). This requires applying some basic *search engine optimization* (SEO) skills and including keywords in your content, for both Facebook and overall organic searches, so your Page can be found through the site and on the Internet at large.

Organic Search

Facebook Pages are indexed by search engines. Facebook even has deals with Google and Bing to pull its social content for a feature called *real-time search*. Your Page will be visible in search results, provided you have optimized it correctly, and can even be viewed by people who do not have a Facebook account.

Facebook Search

Facebook's internal site search is notoriously picky, but it is getting better. As you might imagine, ranking well in an internal Facebook search is even more important (Figure 3-10). Someone searching for your brand directly within Facebook knows what she wants and is almost certain to click Like when she reaches your Page.

When optimizing your Facebook Page, focus primarily on keywords and content; Facebook adds the *nofollow* attribute to links, making it difficult to pass on any link power. A good, keyword-rich content strategy should be at the heart of your Page optimization plan, as it will help new users find you and keep old ones coming back. Of course, also include all the important links to your site so that people who like you on Facebook can easily navigate to your website.

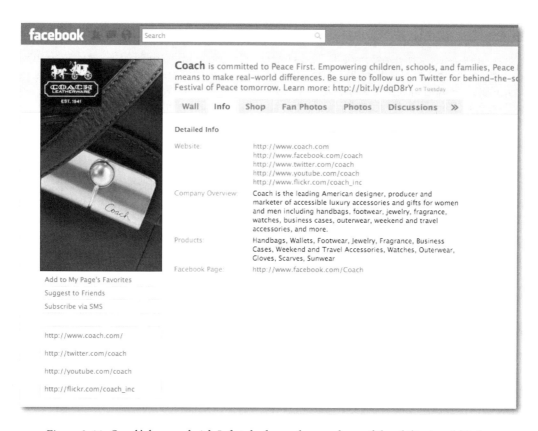

Figure 3-11. Coach's keyword-rich Info tab also makes good use of the ability to add links.

Page Optimization Tips

Optimizing your Page begins with setup and continues throughout your Facebook marketing strategy. The tips below will help you start your Page on the right path and enable you to better optimize later through content and design.

Pick a descriptive Page name and URL.

Choose a good Page name (usually your brand name or tagline) and encourage 25 people to like the Page quickly in order to secure your vanity URL. This URL will be in the form of Facebook.com/ *YourPageName*, so choose something easy to remember and closely tied to your brand.

Fill out the Info section completely.

Make sure you take your time and choose the right category for your Page. The category you choose affects what and how much you can add to the Info tab. Fill out the Info section completely, and use a lot of keywords. Also add all of your related websites, including your blog, online store, and Twitter page (Figure 3-11).

Use the About box.

One of the most undervalued and overlooked features of a Facebook Page is that little box on the left, below the Page's picture. Prominently displayed on the Wall tab, this box is a great place to add keywords to quickly signal what your Page is about to both users and search engines. Plus, you can add a clickable link. Just be careful not to exceed the box's 250-character limit.

These tips will help you optimize your Page during setup. To keep it up to date, ranking highly, and attracting new members, however, you also need an ongoing content strategy.

Figure 3-12. Look for multiple ways to cross-promote content, such as on a Facebook tab, Facebook Wall, and website.

Optimizing Through a Content Strategy

To maintain your rankings and drive new traffic to your Page, you need to constantly populate the Page with new content through both automated and manual postings.

Cross-promote content.

> Go beyond just including a link to your website and connect all your web properties with automated applications wherever possible (Figure 3-12). RSS feeds from a blog or Twitter, for example, can post to your Wall as well as a custom tab. This keeps a steady stream of new content coming in, with links back to your site, without a lot of extra effort.

Encourage engagement.

> An important part of a content strategy is driving interactions. Each interaction on your Page, whether in the form of liking or commenting, functions as a vote for your Page. The more engagement and interaction on your Page, the higher it ranks. This also keeps it in your members' newsfeeds; as they interact with new items, their friends will see this and be drawn to your Page.

Keep content flowing.

> The most important part of a content strategy is to keep it going! No one will interact with a stagnant Page, and many will click Unlike if you don't deliver. An automated RSS feed can help, but be sure to add some Facebook-specific content as well. This is where you can really drive engagement by asking people to comment on photos as part of a promotion or by developing timely, targeted articles that encourage sharing. And above all else, respond to Page members on your Wall.

Figure 3-13. A variety of promotional tactics, incentives, and continuous new content keeps the Victoria's Secret Pink Page fresh and engaging.

Promoting Your Page

You've set up your Page and created a custom tab, and optimized content is flowing. Now it's time to promote your Page and convince people to like it. The best promotions incorporate a combination of paid, organic, and incentive offers. Try to use all three; just make sure your Page is ready to be unveiled before you start asking people to join.

Paid advertising

Pure and simple: you could buy a Facebook ad. In fact, Facebook hopes you will become not just a brand, but also an advertiser. If you have a little money and want to gain members quickly, this might be an avenue to pursue. Just don't rely on it by itself.

Organic promotion

Put links to your Facebook Page on your website and add them to the header or footer of emails you send to your email list. Better yet, write a blog post about the new Page and send an email to all your subscribers informing them that your new Facebook Page is live. Many people probably have been waiting for this; make an event of the launch, and then place permanent links on the site and all future email communications.

Incentive offers

We all love free stuff. Offer exclusive information, deals, or discounts just to members of your Facebook Page (Figure 3-13). Add this incentive to your launch email or blog post to give people an even better reason to click Like. You don't need to go crazy with giveaways, but be ready to offer something.

Figure 3-14. Wall posts, status updates, and user comments on the Zappos Page encourage interaction.

Page Interactions

There are many ways that users can interact with your Page, from the ongoing stream of status updates and posts that appear on the Wall to media uploads they can comment on. Custom applications, especially those designed for user interaction, also encourage clicking. Every interaction works to improve your ranking and keep your name high up in the Facebook Newsfeed.

Wall posts

The preferred means of communication for frequent Facebook users is Wall posting, because these messages are quick and easy to post (Figure 3-14). They are also open and visible to the public—great for praise, but not so much for complaints. Be sure to respond quickly here.

Media comments

Members of your Page can view and comment on anything you upload to the Page. Take photos at events to encourage liking and tagging when people see themselves, and consider a photo comment contest to get engagement going, especially early on.

Inbox updates

These messages won't help your Page interaction directly, but you can use them to bulk-message all Page members and alert them to important new uploads. Include links to send members directly to the content you want them to interact with.

Custom applications

As you design your custom application, be sure to think socially. Provide easy ways for users to share the results of your application with friends or invite them to try it as well. Include a Share button at all stages of interaction with the application so users can post to their Wall and newsfeed.

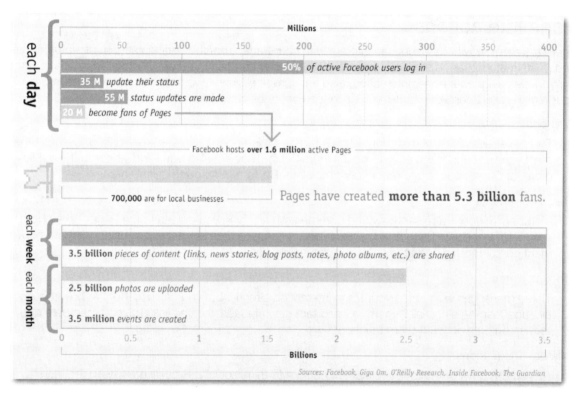

Figure 3-15. Facebook hosts over 1.6 million active Pages, with a combined total of 5.3 billion Page members. (Graphic by Muhammad Saleem for Mashable.com.)

Summary

According to Facebook, there are nearly 500 million active Facebook users, each of whom is connected to 60 Facebook Pages, Groups, and Events on average. The popular Facebook-focused blog All Facebook keeps a running tally of the most popular Facebook Pages, ranked by the number of users who like these Pages. At this writing, the top Page is Zynga's Texas Hold'em Poker, with more than 17 million user connections, while the official Page for Facebook is approaching 10 million.

Obviously, Facebook is growing rapidly (Figure 3-15), as are Facebook Pages. Pages are the key to your brand's marketing on Facebook. Whether your goals are search presence, general awareness, customer service, or sales, you need to take this social network seriously if you want your Page to succeed.

More and more, Facebook users are expecting brands to be on Facebook. They look at the site much the way we looked at the Internet 10 years ago, and are confused when they can't find their favorite store or celebrity. Don't disappoint your fans with a half-hearted Page. Think of your Facebook Page as an extension of your website and put the same amount of time and effort into it.

CHAPTER 4

Facebook Group Basics

Facebook Groups are often set up by fans of a brand, as is the case with the extremely popular Coke bottle Groups that exclaim how much better a bottle is than a can. Groups are much faster and easier to create than Pages, which is why many fans are quick to set them up, but they also offer less functionality.

Most of your Facebook marketing efforts should stem from a Facebook Page; Pages are the official channel for brands to reach consumers, as determined by Facebook. Overall, they offer more functionality and better opportunities to interact with members. Still, there is some value in using Groups for occasional marketing efforts. To help you make the best decisions for your campaign, this chapter explains where Groups came from and examines how and when you should take advantage of them.

	Groups	Pages
Mass Messaging	✓*	✕
Indexed By Google	✓	✓
Stream Publishing	✓	✓
Targeted Stream Posts	✕	✓
Targeted Updates	✕	✓
Support For Applications	✕	✓
Membership Restrictions	✓	✕
Event Inbox Messaging	✓	✕
Engagement Metrics	✕	✓
Promotional Widgets	✕	✓
Vanity URLs	✕	✓

*messaging is restricted once a group grows past 5,000 members

Source: AllFacebook.com

Figure 4-1. As this chart by All Facebook shows, Group functionality can vary greatly from that of Pages.

Groups Versus Pages

Facebook Groups were the first organized way for marketers to message their audience. They were quick and easy to set up but provided little to no engagement or customization. Facebook has come a long way since then, but many differences between Pages and Groups still exist (Figure 4-1).

Pages are the Facebook-preferred method of corporation-to-consumer interaction. In fact, Facebook's intention is so clear that when the site first introduced Pages, Facebook itself took on the work of converting many official brand Groups into Pages. By migrating power-players such as Apple, Facebook hoped that users would learn to like Pages and quickly prefer them to Groups.

Pages are intended to help create relationships with customers or brand evangelists and are better for long-term messaging, while Groups are centered on discussions and more temporary topics. For that very reason, however, creating a Group is preferable in many situations to using a Page. Groups work well when you want to take quick action around a time-sensitive issue, and they're often used to rally people around causes or current events. They can also be effective as offshoots or subsections of your Page.

Figure 4-2. Photo albums are very popular with Groups because they bring a more human element that Pages lack. This local Group posts photos of members at events.

Groups were intended to facilitate organization and discussion around a particular topic, and they still provide a more open space for such conversations. Pages lack the personal aspect Groups excel at; joining in a Group feels more like belonging than just liking a Page does (Figure 4-2). Groups are also often much more targeted than Pages, which gives them a more active and engaged member base.

More Personal Messaging

Groups can have an unlimited number of members, but you can message members only as long as the Group has a membership of fewer than 5,000 people. Those messages are very powerful, because Group messages are sent directly to members' inboxes, just like messages from a friend. A Page admin can send only Page updates that go to a separate, more hidden inbox specifically for Page messages.

Better Event Management

Because Groups are maintained by real people, they are better suited for managing Events and have more Event functionality, such as messaging attendees. Group content is also now included in the Facebook Newsfeed, something once exclusive to Pages. This is a major factor in retaining members and driving engagement.

Groups are not, however, able to customize as much content, add applications, or select a vanity URL. This prevents them from ranking as highly in a search. Facebook also continues to more heavily support Pages through promotion widgets, ads, and development resources dedicated to improving Pages for both admins and users.

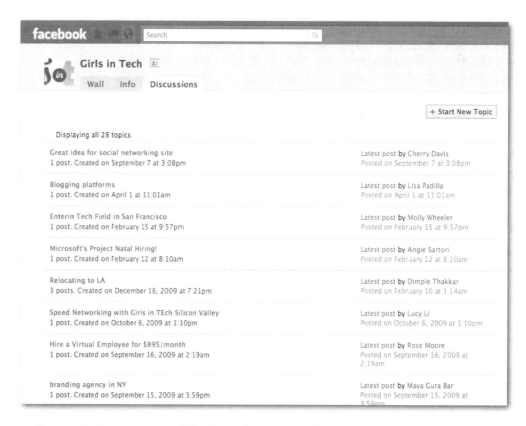

Figure 4-3. Groups are intended to foster discussion, as this one does with technology topics.

Groups Can Be Good—Sometimes

Groups do have some value. They're quick and easy to set up—great when you're in a pinch, but not so great because of all the spammy, discarded Groups that litter Facebook searches. The ease of use for Groups is what makes them appealing, but also what makes them seem untrustworthy.

While a Page may seem daunting to manage, a Group can be an easier way to transition into Facebook marketing. Unlike Pages, Groups allow their admins to send out mass invites to join a Group. Again, fast and easy but also annoying. When something big hits fast, Groups can be great, but you should not use them for an overall, long-term marketing strategy.

So when is it OK to use a Group? According to Facebook,"Groups and Pages serve different purposes on Facebook. Groups are meant to foster Group discussion around a particular topic area, while Pages allow entities such as public figures and organizations to broadcast information to their fans. Only the authorized representative of the entity can run a Page" (Figure 4-3).

Facebook has also started to offer additional functionality for Groups, making them appear more like Pages and displaying content in the Facebook Newsfeed. While this might sound like good news to some, a large Group can quickly become unwieldy, and many admins are finding it easier to message Group members to switch to liking their Pages instead.

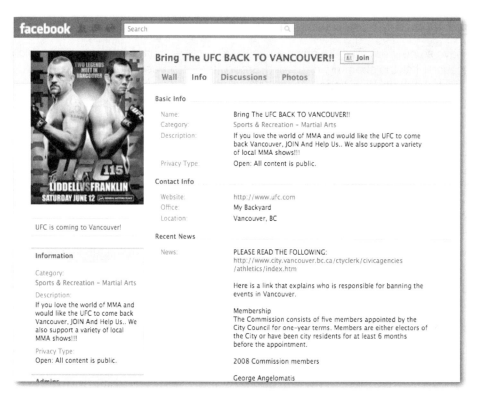

facebook   Search   🔍

Bring The UFC BACK TO VANCOUVER!!   🔲 Join

Wall   **Info**   Discussions   Photos

Basic Info

Name:	Bring The UFC BACK TO VANCOUVER!!
Category:	Sports & Recreation - Martial Arts
Description:	If you love the world of MMA and would like the UFC to come back Vancouver, JOIN And Help Us.. We also support a variety of local MMA shows!!!
Privacy Type:	Open: All content is public.

Contact Info

Website:	http://www.ufc.com
Office:	My Backyard
Location:	Vancouver, BC

Recent News

News: PLEASE READ THE FOLLOWING:
http://www.city.vancouver.bc.ca/ctyclerk/civicagencies/athletics/index.htm

Here is a link that explains who is responsible for banning the events in Vancouver.

Membership
The Commission consists of five members appointed by the City Council for one-year terms. Members are either electors of the City or have been city residents for at least 6 months before the appointment.

2008 Commission members

George Angelomatis

UFC is coming to Vancouver!

Information

Category:
Sports & Recreation – Martial Arts

Description:
If you love the world of MMA and would like the UFC to come back Vancouver, JOIN And Help Us.. We also support a variety of local MMA shows!!!

Privacy Type:
Open: All content is public.

Admins

Figure 4-4. Rallying people to take action is often easier to achieve with a Group, like this one hoping to bring the UFC back to Vancouver.

When You Want a Group

Groups are often faster and easier to set up than Pages. They also offer a more personalized and controlled atmosphere for conversation. As a marketing tool, a Group is a better option when:

Time is a factor.

Groups are helpful for time-sensitive initiatives (Figure 4-4) that need to reach critical mass quickly. In a global Group, any Group member can send bulk invites to his friends, which can be helpful for viral marketing. Beware of overusing this feature, however, as those invites may be perceived as spam.

You need control.

Groups also offer more control over who is allowed in or out, while Pages are open to everyone. A Group can be open just to a particular school or work network, or to all of Facebook. You can also require permission for joining a Group so that everyone must be approved by an admin (but can see some Group content before requesting to join), or you can make the Group completely secret and visible only to those you invite. This makes Groups helpful as a separate subsection of your Page, perhaps for your biggest brand supporters.

It's personal.

All around, Facebook Groups provide a feeling of more personal interaction. Groups are directly tied to the person who administers them, and that Profile name will appear on the Group, unlike a more anonymous Page, which could be manned by any number of people. Some find this personal connection a welcome change in the digital world, especially when dealing with more sensitive topics or emotional issues, like health questions or life-changing events.

Figure 4-5. You can fine-tune a lot of the settings for your Group. Keep them global and open to maximize your reach.

Creating a Group

When you need to promote something quickly or are looking to foster a stronger sense of community, a Facebook Group may be the way to go. To create a Group, go to the Groups application and click Create a Group in the upper-right corner of the Page. All Groups require a Group name, description, and Group type. You cannot edit the network of a Group after it is created, so think carefully before you begin.

Keep It Global

To get the maximum reach and value out of your Group, you need to ensure that anyone who wants to can join without having to be approved by an admin. You also want them to be able to invite their friends, as this cuts down on the work for you and allows you to focus on building content that people want to share. When setting up your Group, make sure you create it as a Global Group (Figure 4-5) so it is visible to all of Facebook, and set its access to Open, allowing members to invite friends. Members should also be able to post and share links and media on the Group Page. On the other hand, if you are using a Group specifically for its privacy controls, you may wish to keep the Group closed so you can approve members.

Figure 4-6. Provide a detailed description of your Group, and be sure to include links and keywords. This will help people find the Group and convince them to join right away.

Fill Out All Fields

As with Pages, you should include as much information as possible when setting up your Group (Figure 4-6). This thoroughness is what truly separates a successful, professional Group from a spammy, I-lost-my-phone, give-me-your-numbers Group. Don't go overboard with lengthy text—stick to basic web-reading principles—but don't leave anything blank, including the image field.

Use Proper Grammar, Punctuation, and Spelling

Setting up a Group may be faster than creating a Page, but it requires the same amount of care. The biggest tip-offs that a Group was hastily put together are spelling and grammar errors. If a potential member's first impression of your Group is that it's full of errors, she will assume future content won't provide much value either. Proofread your description.

Include Keywords for Easier Searching

Groups don't provide as much content to crawl as a Page, but they are indexed by search engines as well as by Facebook searches. When filling out your Group description, be sure to include keywords. This increases the chance that a potential member will find your Group while searching for similar topics, organizations, or events. The same goes for creating a Group name; think of keywords people would associate with your content or the purpose of the Group.

- Wendy Schreider (Boston, MA)
- Natasha Lewin
- Kirsten Lundeen
- Dorota Spaulding (Cambridge Associates)
- Jenn Schumann
- Allison Dalton Griffin (Boston, MA)
- Aaron MacDaniel (Babson) (creator)

Officers

Dorota Spaulding (Cambridge Associates)
Chair

Rich Hornblower
Vice Chair

Jessica Fischburg
Secretary & SHA Representative

Allison Dalton Griffin (Boston, MA)
SED Representative

Wendy Schreider (Boston, MA)
CGS Representative

Nabil Aidoud (Boston, MA)
ENG Representative

Natasha Lewin
SMG Representative

Kelly Mizer
SAR Representative

Phyllis Ottaviano (Bridgeport / Stamford, CT)
MED Representative

Members

6 of 1,143 members   See All

Heather Papsun
Seth Needle
Kate Yenrick

Jessica Fischburg YAC is switching from a group to a page– please "Like" us!

Boston University Young Alumni
The Young Alumni Club (YAC) is a group dedicated to all BU alumni, from any school or college, who have graduated within the past fifteen years. The YAC provides young alumni in the greater Boston area with the opportunity to continue to come together for social, educat...

Non-Profit: 579 people like this.

See More

August 19 at 10:31pm · Comment · Like · Share · Flag

Sarah Bormel and Darcey Searles like this.

Write a comment...

BU Young Alumni Club (YAC) Join the YAC for our August Planning Meeting to discuss upcoming events and more!

The meeting is held on the 7th floor of SMG– please enter through the side entrance. Light dinner will be served.

After the meeting, we will head to 973 Comm Ave (formerly T's Pub) for some karaoke! Karaoke get's kicked off around 10pm.
...
See More

YAC August Planning Meeting & Karaoke at T's Pub!
Tuesday, August 10, 2010 at 6:30pm
7th Floor of SMG followed by 973 Commonwealth Ave

July 28 at 9:46am · Comment · Like · Share

Jessica Fischburg

Figure 4-7. The BU Young Alumni Group is a good example of a Group that is connected to a Page and really focuses on building a community for alumni.

Managing a Group

Once your Group is set up correctly, you need to start adding members and posting content. Read Chapter 9 for more ideas on posting, and keep in mind that the goal of a Group is to start conversations. Many of your duties as an admin will center on monitoring discussions and encouraging comments where necessary (Figure 4-7).

Use with Profile or Page

When Facebook first introduced Pages, it offered Group admins the option of automatically transitioning members into fans. As a result, many brands now have a single presence on Facebook, in the form of a Page. To launch a Group, however, you need a *parent* Profile—that is, the Profile of a single person who will administer the Group. The parent Profile gives you a base from which to invite people and provide that human connection.

Don't Make New Friends

Since a Group cannot exist on its own, you'll use your Profile to invite at least the first batch of members. That makes it tempting to start sending random friend requests to a bunch of people you don't know. Inviting unknown members goes against Facebook's Terms of Service and will very quickly get you banned. If you do want to add a few new people, make sure you include a personal message in your potential friend request explaining how you found them and why you want to be friends.

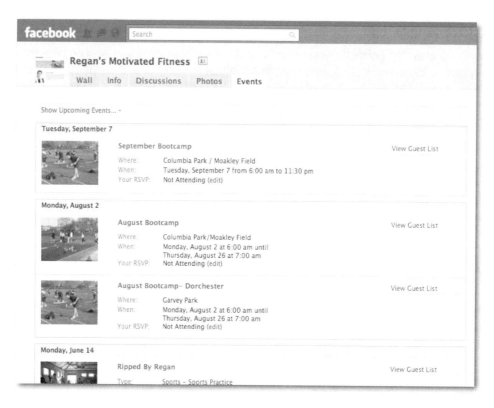

Figure 4-8. Groups are a great place to post events, both real and virtual. This local gym uses Group events to motivate members.

Segment Friend Lists

If you use your Profile to invite the first few Group members, it will be helpful to segment your friends into relevant lists for future marketing purposes. You can label people as already invited (so you know not to try again) or based on their interests. If you run a restaurant, for example, make a list for your vegetarian friends so you can message them with special information about vegetarian meals and specials.

Incorporate Events

Events and Groups have a greater reach than other elements on Facebook, as they have built-in pass-it-on functionality (Figure 4-8). Include a brief introduction with your Event invite and keep it as open as possible. Allow guests to invite other people and post their own videos, links, and photos. These can be physical or virtual events, just like with a Page.

Send Messages

Group messaging is more useful than Facebook Page messaging, because Group messages are delivered to the recipient's inbox just like those from friends. You can quickly keep all members up-to-date on Group news, events, and information by selecting Message All Members and drafting your message like any other private correspondence on Facebook. Keep in mind that this works only if your Group has fewer than 5,000 members. But when you use Message All Members in conjunction with your segmented friend lists, you can deliver very targeted, relevant messaging.

Figure 4-9. Some Groups, like this one that helps members reminisce about the '90s, naturally get a lot of posts. Others may require more encouragement from admins.

Participate and Post New Content

Unlike Pages, Groups can have many separate privacy settings. For maximum engagement and effectiveness, you want to keep the Group Wall, photo, and video restrictions open to encourage content sharing and discussion. Groups are centered on conversation, and you need to keep the discussion going. But allowing posts will only get you so far—post thought-starter questions and links yourself.

To create a Group that retains members, particularly engaged members, you need to keep the content fresh. A Facebook Page can be automatically updated. For your Group to compete, you need to provide interesting, valuable perspectives or information to members.

Post Links, Photos, Videos

Besides providing fresh content, frequent posting keeps members engaged and allows for greater interaction (Figure 4-9). Post links to external sites or to other parts of Facebook, and ask questions about the content found there, like in a book club. You can also post photos or videos on related topics or from actual real-life Group events.

Group functionality is limited, so make the most of what you've got. Groups are set up more like Profiles, so photos, links, and videos are the best ways to bring in external content or brand look and feel. This means that you will rely on content for customizing a Group and breaking through the clutter. Remember to keep the discussion going and post frequently.

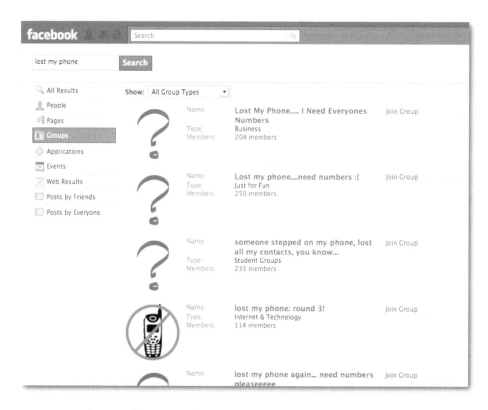

Figure 4-10. The ease of creating and posting on Groups makes them a target for spammers. Monitor closely and remove offensive or unrelated posts.

Monitoring and Managing a Group

A Group admin controls the membership and content of a Group. As an admin, you can send messages to the Group, appoint other admins and officers, and edit Group info and settings. You can also remove current members and remove inappropriate posts or uploads.

You may have fewer opportunities to customize a Group, but the lack of applications to interact with and showcase content actually means you'll have to monitor and moderate the Group more carefully. The only interaction people can have with a Group is to post content, so there's a higher likelihood you will need to answer questions or remove spam (Figure 4-10).

Removing Content

Develop a removal or response strategy, just like for a Page. Be ready to remove posts that use foul language or are overly hateful to your Group's goal. Also watch for bullying of other members, as well as people who post unrelated spam content to the Group Wall.

Encouraging Posting

Managing a Group isn't just about removing inappropriate posts. You need to keep the content flowing and the conversation engaging. Hopefully, your Group will be full of useful content from members. But if not, part of your job will be to push them toward posting by asking questions, making introductions, and posting links to interesting articles or sites.

Figure 4-11. This Facebook Group connects Boston University Alumni, a subset of the entire Boston University faculty, student, and alumni community.

Using Groups to Supplement Your Page

If you like all the bells and whistles of a Facebook Page but appreciate the discussion aspect of a Group as well, try doing both. You'll get the search engine optimization (SEO) and brand buzz benefits of a Page, as well as the ability to design tabs and develop applications, but you'll also be able to create a smaller, community-based presence within your Group (Figure 4-11).

Pages allow you to target posts to geographic areas, but a Group enables you to target people based on interests. A restaurant chain, for example, could have a Page for its overall brand and Groups for each individual location. People can belong to one or both, allowing them to see general news and promotions from the Page, as well as local updates and conversations about menu items and events.

You could also have a secret Group where you invite only your best customers and post special sales, promo codes, or sneak peeks of content. Or watch for topics that take off on your Page and create Groups around them. If a lot of people are posting about healthy food options on your restaurant Page, start a Group just for them. Talk about your healthier options, and how they can modify orders to cut calories without losing the restaurant experience.

There are many ways to use a Group as a companion to a Page. Take direction from your members, and be willing to experiment.

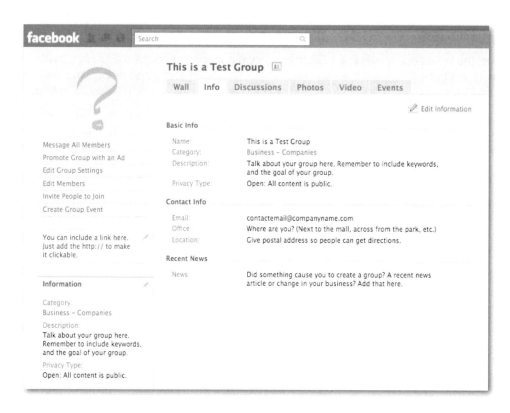

Figure 4-12. Groups can be quick to set up, but you've got to do it right. Always keep the conversation flowing and encourage participation.

Summary

Facebook Groups are well suited for marketing around time-sensitive issues and causes. Groups have a more close-knit feel and are a little bit simpler to grasp than Pages. The ease of use and intuitive communication tools make them a great place to provide an open forum for members.

Remember, Group participation starts with the admin. Ask questions to get people talking, offering stories, and sharing tips. Be careful when this involves sensitive topics or health issues. You don't want false information or family remedies taking over your Group. If that is a concern, a closed Group will allow you to approve people before they join and post.

A lot of elements go into even the simplest of Groups (Figure 4-12), but Facebook offers tools to help you. Your challenge is to use them correctly. The most important thing you can remember is that people only get out of a Group what you put in. Take the time to set it up right, and actively monitor and participate in your Group.

CHAPTER 5

Facebook Events

Using Facebook's Event functions, you can invite users to any event, be it real or virtual. Events are great for rallying Page members around a timely happening, whether it is a sale, movie opening, menu revamp, or new product launch. Plus, because Events have a dedicated tab on your Page, Page members can easily see what you're up to.

Events are quick and easy to set up, perfect for creating a quick response to a time-sensitive issue. This makes them a no-brainer for inclusion in your Facebook marketing strategy. On the flip side, they are also easy enough for anyone else to make, leaving a lot of Event clutter on the site. This makes it harder (but not impossible) to use Facebook Events effectively. You just need a little extra effort to make your Event stand out.

Figure 5-1. Facebook Events should be used for actual events that include a time and a place in the real world. They can also be used for virtual events, but be careful not to confuse people.

When to Use an Event

The best way to use an Event is as you would use a printed invitation: when you have an actual event to promote (Figure 5-1). Using Facebook to send event information is a lot faster (and cheaper) than printing and mailing invitations to all your contacts.

Facebook Events can also make a great accompaniment to an email announcement or an actual invitation. You may want to send select people an announcement or invitation to a store opening through the postal mail (like restaurant reviewers or fashion bloggers) and then follow up with the more general population online. Your various contact lists will most likely overlap, but it's wise to message people in different ways to ensure a large turnout. Send an email announcement about an upcoming sale, then follow up with a Facebook Event invitation as the date draws near.

It's OK to create a Facebook Event for every real-life happening you host. If you have a lot of parties, sales, or promotions, you definitely want to use the Events tab on your Facebook Page to promote them. Don't go overboard with actually inviting people or messaging Page members, however. Just because you created an Event doesn't mean you need to invite everyone you've ever met. That's a surefire way to drive unlikes of your Page.

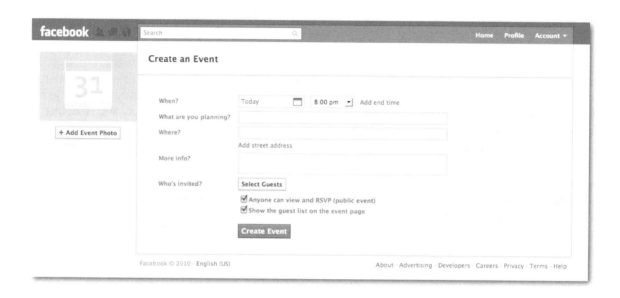

Figure 5-2. Give guests as much information as possible when creating an Event.
Fill out every field completely—they're there for a reason.

Creating an Event

Setting up a Facebook Event (Figure 5-2) is one of the easiest things to do on the site. Perhaps that's why there are so many unfinished and unmonitored Events littering the social network. Don't contribute to the mess: create your Events correctly.

Keep Your Event Public

Make your Event searchable. Use search engine optimization principles to come up with a name, and include keywords in the Event description. Think of popular searches or topics that might appeal to people whom you want to attend.

Allow Interaction

Keep your Event as open as possible. One way to do this is to allow your invitees to invite other people. This opens up your Event to a much larger network. Allow all your invitees to post videos, links, and photos of the Event. You can use this strategy to drive interest leading up to the big night and to grab content for your Page afterward, when attendees are likely to post photos they took at the Event. Encourage conversation among invitees by keeping the Wall open to allow discussion. Don't forget to participate yourself!

Figure 5-3. To break through the clutter of random Facebook Events, be sure to upload an image, check for proper grammar, and include lots of keywords.

Breaking Through the Clutter

A lot of people use Events for things like lost phones and silly surveys (Figure 5-3), so correct setup is key to Facebook Event success. Events are very easy to spread because other people can pass them on and invite people from outside the original creator's network. This easy transfer also means, however, that users may be exposed to many Event messages on a daily basis.

Because most users have caught on to how easy it is to create an Event, you'll have to make yours better than all those pesky phone-number requests. Luckily, most of these "throwaway" Events are riddled with typos and not hard to outdo. Here are a few tips to break through the Event clutter:

Upload an image.

> The first giveaway that an Event is likely to be a bust is the blank calendar graphic, the Event equivalent of the question mark Profile picture. Upload an inviting image, and you're already ahead of the game.

Fill out all fields.

> Accurately describe your Event. This will help with search results, while also demonstrating that there is value to attending your Event.

Respond to invitees.

> Actively participating in pre- and post-event discussions will help keep people excited and increase the chances of their attending.

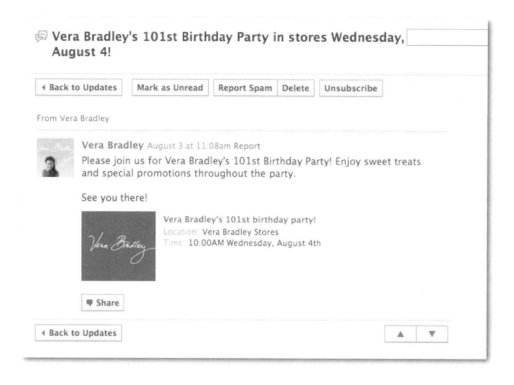

Figure 5-4. Because Facebook limits the number of Event invitations you can send, it's often easier to send a mass update to all Page members with a link to the Event and let them add themselves to the guest list.

Sending Invites

Now that you've created your Event on Facebook, here's the (slight) catch. As a marketer, you should be using a Page to talk to your fans on Facebook, but a Page can't invite people to an Event. Only a personal Profile has that capability.

You have a few options here. One would be to break the Facebook Terms of Service and create a Facebook Profile for your brand as well. Not only is that not a great idea, but you'll also waste a lot of time and energy. A better solution is to use your own Profile to personally invite some friends you think might be interested in the Event. Start small and encourage them to invite their friends. You can also use your email list to invite people to an Event. This can be tricky, as you can invite only 100 people in one invite blast, and Facebook allows only 300 pending invitations at any given time. Still, your email list can be a great way to seed the Event with some of your major supporters.

The good news is that, although you can invite only 100 people at a time, an unlimited number of people can RSVP to an Event. So you can create a post on your Facebook Page with a link to the Event or send a mass update to Page members (Figure 5-4). As long as you keep the Event open and public, members can simply add themselves to the guest list.

Figure 5-5. A local restaurant uses Facebook Events to promote special dinners, while international clothing retailer Gap advertises its in-store and online sales.

Integrating with a Page

Because most of your Facebook marketing will happen directly on your brand's Page, you'll want to incorporate Events as much as possible. This helps increase attendance and Event success, while also showing Page members that you are committed to building a better Facebook experience for them. Remember, you want to continually give them reasons to interact with the Page.

Use the Event tab.

When you create the Event, make sure you do so from your brand Page and not your personal account. You need to post updates as the brand, not yourself. You also want to make sure that the Event tab is prominently displayed (Figure 5-5). If you don't see it, check the hidden tabs behind the arrows on the right of the Page. From here you can drag Events to a new position in the tabs.

Post the Event link on your Wall.

Include a little tease to the Event, and invite your friends to visit the unique Event URL to add themselves to the guest list. Promote the Event periodically over the days or weeks leading up to the big day, making sure to vary the language you use and the time of day you post in order to maximize visibility and excitement while minimizing fatigue.

Send an update to Page members.

Updates are often overlooked (they are somewhat hidden as a subset of inbox messages), but you should send one out with an Event link, much like the Wall post. It doesn't hurt to message people in different places.

Figure 5-6. A well-designed Facebook Event that was used to announce a virtual live-chat event.

Promoting Your Event

Setting up your Event correctly—including keywords, images, and open invite settings—will go a long way toward organically gaining some attendees (Figure 5-6). While integrating the Event with your Page will promote it to your current audience, promoting your Event outside Facebook can help you attract new Page members and potential customers. Here are some ideas.

Send an email blast.

> Yes, this is still your current customer base, but they may not all be Facebook Page members. Emailing an Event gives them yet another reason to click Like for your Page, while also providing them with a piece of content that is easy to forward to their friends.

Tweet about it.

> Sometimes Twitter and Facebook don't play nicely with each other, but in this case, it's OK to promote a Facebook feature on Twitter. Facebook is really just your landing page. Tweet a link to the Event (be sure to use a URL shortener) and encourage people to retweet and invite their friends.

Link it from your site.

> If you're going to host a lot of Events, you should integrate those announcements somehow. Add a page to your website just for Events, and direct site visitors to Facebook to sign up for the Facebook Event there. This way, you won't end up with two guest lists or require users to sign up for a separate site to RSVP.

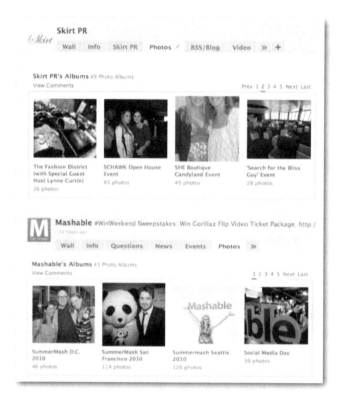

Figure 5-7. A fashion-focused PR firm always makes sure to take photos at an event and upload them to clearly labeled Facebook albums. The popular social media blog Mashable does the same at its real-life events.

Event Follow-Up

At the Event, you'll get a chance to meet some fans of your brand. After it's over, you should have some great content and stories to share with them. Post this content to your Event page so that attendees can see their photos, and people who couldn't attend this time can see what they missed. A few simple uploads will keep them engaged with your brand and also help you immediately begin building excitement for the next Event.

Post photos and video.

> Upload any media you gathered at the Event to both your brand Page and the unique Event Page. Make sure every Event has its own photo album, video, or both on your brand Page, and clearly label and explain the Event (Figure 5-7). You can also link to the Facebook Event Page. Adding photos creates social proof and tells people your Events are fun and worth going to. It also keeps attendees engaged as they try to tag themselves in photos and share with friends.

Send a thank-you note.

> Say thanks for attending in the form of both a status update on your Page and a mass update to Page members. It's a nice touch and a courtesy that still applies in the digital age. You can also link to the photos from your Event and encourage attendees to tag photos and comment on their favorite part of the night.

Use what you got.

> Use the photos and comments from one Event when you plan the next one. Include mentions of "the last time" so attendees remember how much fun they had and to entice newcomers to get in on the action.

Figure 5-8. *The Starbucks Frappuccino Happy Hour was a widely promoted nationwide event that included a public Facebook Event component.*

Summary

The ease of Event setup creates a lot of spammy or poorly written Facebook Events. You can break through the clutter with proper punctuation and grammar, informative Event information, and an eye-catching image. Also, keep your setting public for maximum Event visibility (Figure 5-8).

To ensure your Event is a success—in real life and on Facebook—use your other marketing channels in conjunction with it. Make the most of this simple and free Facebook tool. Promote the Event to your email list and on your Facebook Page. Don't just expect people to find the Event and invite their friends. Make sure they know what's going on, when it's happening, and that you want them to bring friends.

CHAPTER 6

Facebook Application Basics

Several years ago, Facebook released a platform that allowed developers to create applications to leverage the site's features and the social information of its users. When a user installs or *adds* your application, the app can display content on his Profile, as well as gain limited access to his information. For marketers, applications present an opportunity to create engaging, branded experiences that are inherently social.

This chapter details what you need to know to brainstorm an idea for a great application, as well as how to plan for its development. To build an application, of course, you'll need development resources. You could task a programmer at your company, hire one, or learn how to code yourself. Any competent developer can learn to work with the Facebook API, but it is not within the scope of this book to teach you to program.

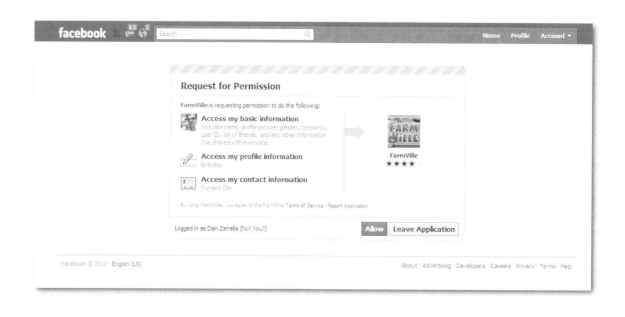

Figure 6-1. When users install your application, the application asks them for permission to access pieces of their personal information.

Create Inherently Social Applications

"Make it go viral!" You've heard the command, but what does it really mean? Confusion about social and viral marketing is frustratingly common. Viral is an outcome; it is the result of the successful release of a contagious campaign. Contagiousness is not something that can be tacked on as an afterthought, but the applications with the greatest chance of *going viral* tend to be the ones that are inherently social.

While it can be a jarring experience when an application abruptly asks a user to invite others (Figure 6-1), the value or enjoyment a user gets from a truly social application often comes directly from her interaction with other people within the app.

Improve Existing Social Behaviors

Facebook itself has been described as a social utility, rather than a social network, in that it is not a collection of people who interact, but a collection of tools that allow people to interact with their existing social networks. For many, Facebook is not a place to meet new people; it is a place to connect and communicate with those they already know. Users were interacting with their social circle long before Facebook existed, and many interactions still happen offline. Facebook is a tool that makes it easier to connect with people over long distances or about specific activities or pieces of content (like the photos of the party we all just attended).

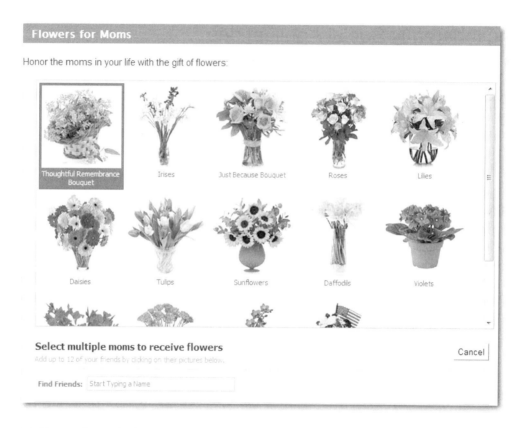

Figure 6-2. Flowers for Mother's Day is a great example of an application that enhances existing social behavior.

One of the easiest ways to design an inherently social application is to identify pre-existing social behavior and make it better. A user is much more likely to use your application to send congratulations to a college graduate than in an entirely new kind of social interaction. The latter is entirely possible—it's just much harder from a motivation and marketing point of view. In fact, one of the most popular applications on Facebook allows users to send one another birthday greetings, an activity as old as birth itself.

Knowing your target audience can help immensely with this. For instance, if you're targeting mothers, you could create an application that allows their children to send them virtual flowers on Mothers' Day (Figure 6-2). Or, if you want to reach new parents, you might build an It's a Boy/Girl application. Even a limited amount of research or knowledge about your prospective users should allow you to create a list of popular, pre-existing social interactions they have on Facebook. Once you've got a list of those actions, decide which fit best with your brand strategy. A cleaning products company would do well to build a party-related application with a reminder that they can help clean up the next morning. If you have an email list of customers, a simple survey asking them what they currently do on Facebook is a quick and easy way to get a ton of great ideas.

Remember that no one wants to socialize about something they perceive as boring (no matter how fascinating you may find life insurance). They want to socialize around themselves and their friends. Work hard to position your brand as the one that helps them do that better.

Figure 6-3. Vampires is a successful application that learned from previous successes on Facebook, including Zombies.

Learn from Success

Stretching the viral marketing metaphor, you might think of contagious Facebook applications as actual, living organisms. If you wished to create a new dog with a certain set of characteristics, you would select parents with those traits and breed them. Similarly, you can borrow features and ideas from successful applications already spreading in the wild and blend them into something new.

In some industries and niches, you'll have one or more direct competitors building applications on Facebook. In most, you won't have this luxury. Rather than look for competitors who are selling products similar to yours, look for companies and applications who are targeting the same audiences you are. In 2007 and 2008, one of the most popular Facebook applications was the virulent Vampires game in which players "bit" their friends to turn them into vampires and gain points (Figure 6-3). Rather than risk a potentially unsuccessful new idea, Sony Pictures rebranded the application to promote their vampire movie *30 Days of Night*. What if you needed to promote a zombie movie? You might try creating a similar zombie application (a few already exist) with your own branded twist.

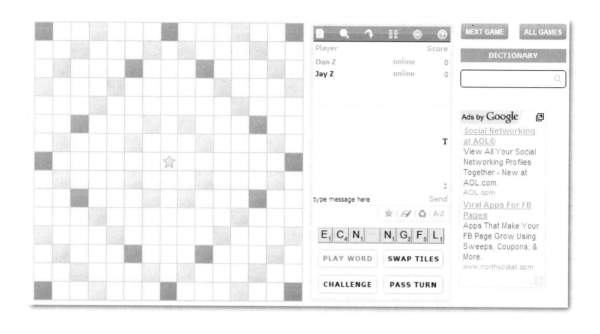

Figure 6-4. Scrabble was successfully and popularly translated from its offline incarnation into a Facebook application.

Approach this borrowing tactic with some caution; you don't want to be seen as merely copying someone else's application. The key is to inject your brand's own special spin into the borrowed concept. A wind power company, for example, could make a wind-farming version of the most popular app on Facebook at the moment: FarmVille. Many popular remix versions of this game already exist and are gaining users daily; check out how PetVille, FishVille, and YoVille built differently on the same idea.

You can also look to successful applications (especially games) outside of Facebook for inspiration. One of the most popular applications ever developed for Facebook was based on the board game Scrabble (Figure 6-4). Don't infringe on a major brand's trademark as the makers of Scrabulous did (and were eventually sued for), but popular card games, nonproprietary board games, and schoolyard sports are all fair game. For example, Zynga's Texas Hold'em poker is an extremely popular application (Figure 6-5).

Figure 6-5. Poker is a social game and the developers of this application built in several touch points where players are encouraged to include their friends.

Clarity, Simplicity, and Speed to Engagement

Remember that your target users are probably already familiar with using Facebook to socialize and aren't super interested in learning a ton of new behaviors. You should strive to make your application as intuitive as possible. One of the most popular Facebook applications of all time is Super Wall, which simply enhanced the existing Wall back before Facebook itself integrated a range of new features. People already understood the concept of a Wall and so there was very little delay from the time they installed the application to the time they were using and enjoying it.

Think of your application in terms of friction and inertia. *Friction* is the amount of time investment, hassle, and commitment a user faces when using an application, and *inertia* is the movitation that user has to push through the friction. If your application is the best thing to happen to Facebook since FarmVille, and everyone knows this to be true, potential users will have enough motivation to deal with a fairly high level of friction. On the other hand, if they've never heard of you or your application, it had better be pretty easy to set up and get value from. Work to reduce friction and increase inertia.

Figure 6-6. Users of your Facebook application can be incentivized to invite their friends to add your application, too.

Integrate with Viral Facebook Features

Facebook is a social network, and as such it contains a wide range of potentially contagious features. Users can invite one another to applications, suggest Pages, send messages, and tag people. Most of these actions trigger Facebook to send messages to the target user informing him of his friend's actions (Figure 6-6). Users can also post updates to their feed, which is displayed on all of their friends' home pages. Be sure your application correctly utilizes these viral features.

Give users reasons to invite their friends, but be careful not to demand or force users to do this. Build in a reason for your application to post to users' feeds. Mafia Wars players get points when they build their crime families by inviting their friends to join the game, and it has become one of the top 20 most popular apps.

Don't fall into the trap of thinking that you can just slap these viral mechanisms onto an app after it's been built. For best results, these mechanisms should be deeply integrated and part of the fundamental reason for using your app. Don't design a Facebook application that functions in a social vaccuum. Build something where the entire point is to interact with other people and spread the app.

Figure 6-7. Your application can display content on users' profiles.

Parts of Your Application

An application has essentially three parts or places on Facebook where you can interact with users: the canvas Page, Profile boxes (Figure 6-7), and your fan Page. The fan Page is a normal Page dedicated to your app, and the functionality there is the same as any other Page. The canvas Page is the central place where users will use your app. Profile boxes are sections of your users' Profiles where you can display some content and functionality.

Development

After you've come up with an awesome idea for your app, draw out exactly how users will interact with it. Don't worry if you don't think you can draw; in fact, the worse you are at making pretty pictures, the better off you'll be when creating mockups. Use a pen and paper (markers work great for this since they force you to forget the details and focus on the overarching structures) or a digital tool such as Balsamiq Mockups, Adobe Photoshop, or even Microsoft PowerPoint. Block out the most important features and user actions and get this mockup in front of potential users as early as you can. Even without a functioning prototype, you'll be surprised at how many great insights you'll get. Draw these fast and don't get too attached to any individual version—you shouldn't be afraid to throw them out and start over.

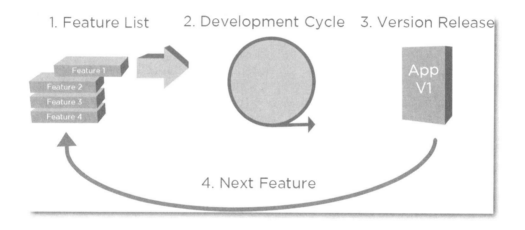

Figure 6-8. The development of a Facebook application should be an iterative, cyclical process.

As mentioned earlier, you probably won't be developing the application yourself. When you're fairly comfortable with your rough mockups, start talking to your developers: they'll give you ideas about how easy or difficult specific parts of your app will be to develop and maintain. You should also start working with your designer at this stage, if you have one separate from your development resources. If you have the resources, it's also a good idea to hire a dedicated user experience and interaction expert.

Facebook is a fluid environment, and you'll be learning as you build and launch your application, so plan to develop in iterations (Figure 6-8). Forget perfectionism; get a minimally functioning application up and running as soon as possible and keep working to improve it. The best development methodology for projects like this is a variant of *agile development*, a subject on which you can find any number of websites or books.

Figure 6-9. Your Facebook application has several places (including its Page) where you'll need to create attractive art and copy to convince users to install it.

Art and Copy

Before you launch the first version of your application, you'll need to craft some images and text (Figure 6-9). The text will be mostly short or microcopy content, including your application's name, a description, and any instructions your users will need to use your app. You'll also need to create an icon. Spend some time and make it good: icons convince users to install and use your application. Think of them in the same iterative ways as your development efforts and strive to constantly improve them.

Launching and Promoting Your Application

When the first usable version of your application is complete, you'll want to start introducing it to potential users. If you have an existing Facebook community, like a Page, those Page members are perfect initial users. Post the app to your Wall. Your Twitter account, blog, or newsletter are also great ways to soft-launch your application to users who already have an affinity for your brand. Listen closely for their feedback and use it to inform the next development iterations you make.

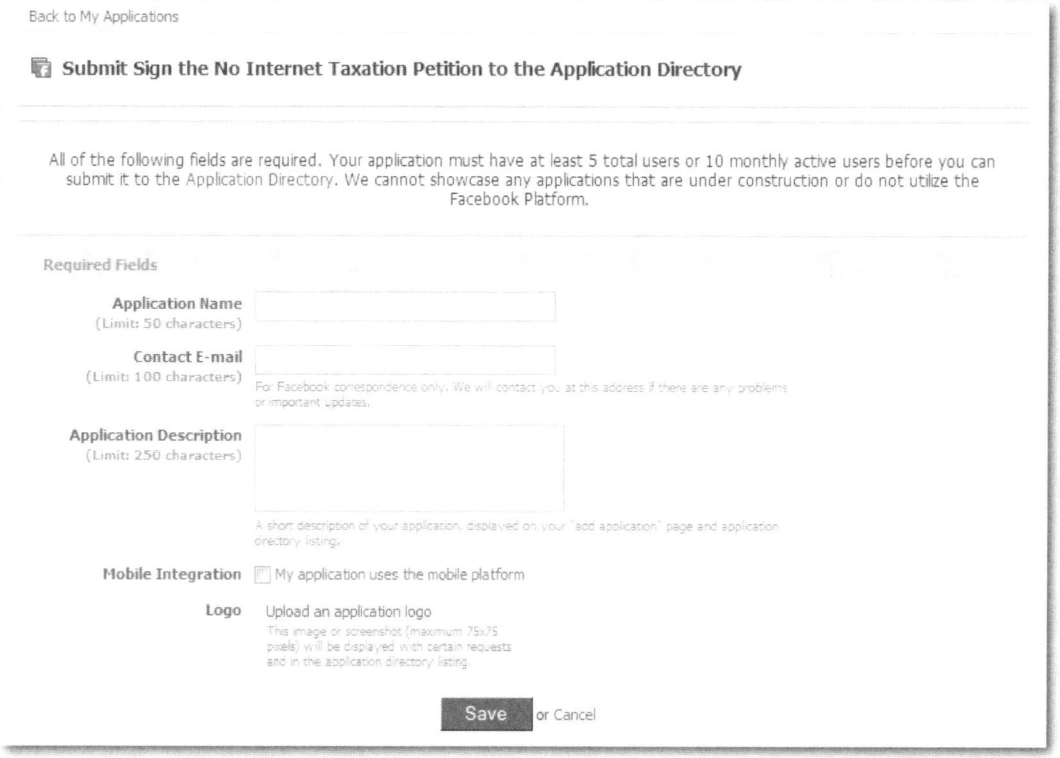

Back to My Applications

Submit Sign the No Internet Taxation Petition to the Application Directory

All of the following fields are required. Your application must have at least 5 total users or 10 monthly active users before you can submit it to the Application Directory. We cannot showcase any applications that are under construction or do not utilize the Facebook Platform.

Required Fields

Application Name
(Limit: 50 characters)

Contact E-mail
(Limit: 100 characters)

For Facebook correspondence only. We will contact you at this address if there are any problems or important updates.

Application Description
(Limit: 250 characters)

A short description of your application, displayed on your "add application" page and application directory listing.

Mobile Integration ☐ My application uses the mobile platform

Logo Upload an application logo
This image or screenshot (maximum 75x75 pixels) will be displayed with certain requests and in the application directory listing.

Save or Cancel

Figure 6-10. This is the screen you'll see when you add your Facebook application to Facebook's Application Directory.

When your application reaches at least 5 total users or 10 monthly active users, you should submit it to Facebook's Application Directory. The link you'll need is on your application's settings Page (Figure 6-10). In addition to the required 250-character description, you can optionally upload a 75-pixel-square logo. Take advantage of both of these opportunities. Describe your application using keywords people are likely to search for and provide an enticing screenshot as your application's logo.

If you designed your application to be inherently social, your soft launch will form a seed of users who will begin sharing it with their friends. In a perfect world, you'll have done such a good job that this seed is all the promotion the app needs to start spreading like wildfire. If that's not the case, don't worry. Remember that you're working iteratively and you'll be constantly making improvements. There are several paid options for promoting your application, the easiest of which is to use Facebook's built-in advertising system (check out Chapter 11 for more information on ads). You can also buy ad space from one of the Facebook application advertising networks, but it is generally a good idea to start with the built-in Facebook ads.

Summary

The most important element of designing a Facebook application is to build social activity directly into the fabric of the application. Don't add on sharing functionality as an afterthought. Figure out what existing social behaviors your target users are performing on Facebook, and use your application to facilitate them.

Minimize the time it takes a user to get value out of your application. Reduce, simplify, and clarify your application so that the experience of using it is as intuitive as possible, and make sure people are being social with your application.

Facebook application development is an ongoing process, and you should strive for the iterative development goals of *release early* and *release often*. Think about your application as a constantly improving work in progress.

CHAPTER 7

Customizing Your Facebook Page

With so many other brands to compete with on Facebook, it's crucial that you customize your Facebook Page. Your best bet for making your content stand out and get shared is to customize every aspect of your Page—from your name and URL to the specific landing tab for new visitors right up to every last status update that current Page members see in their newsfeeds.

Facebook is not as simple to customize as your own site, but you can do a lot even when playing by its rules. Many other brands are not taking full advantage of the free tools and Facebook-provided functionality available to them, so a little extra effort on your part can go a long way. Because Facebook is always changing the exact tools and methods of customization, this chapter explores strategies to make your Page stand out from the rest and become a favorite destination for fans without relying on specific functionality.

Figure 7-1. Longer Facebook icons provide more real estate to customize your Page on the Wall and Info tab. Fashion brands have made good use of this trick.

Page Icon

The Page icon is the first thing current Page members see every time they come to your Page. Its thumbnail image is also how you will be represented in the Facebook Newsfeed, where many other Pages and friends are also clamoring for attention. Your Page icon must stand out but also clearly represent your brand and be easily distinguishable in the fast-paced environment of the Newsfeed.

A Page icon is most often a company logo or some variation of it. The perfect size is 200 pixels square, which shrinks exactly into the thumbnail without cropping. You can also experiment with an elongated icon that is 600 pixels high by 200 pixels wide. In this case, a third of your icon (200 pixels square) should be something that can serve as the thumbnail, and you can specify how Facebook crops the icon. Maintaining a connection between the Page icon and Newsfeed thumbnail will help you increase interaction, engagement, and click-throughs; Page members will immediately recognize your brand in the Newsfeed and respond to your content.

Because the Page icon is such an important representation of your brand and of your Page, you should take full advantage of the space Facebook allows. A longer Page icon gives you more real estate to revamp your Page's look right on the Wall tab, while a consistent logo area within the icon prevents confusion in the Newsfeed. Many fashion brands (Figure 7-1) use a static logo and timely redesigns of the rest of the icon to showcase new looks.

Figure 7-2. A simple custom tab layout helps direct visitors to your site or other parts of Facebook. Keep the look in line with your brand.

Designing Assets and Media

Your Page icon now makes a good first impression, but don't stop there. Take advantage of one of the biggest tools for customization: Facebook tabs. *Display tabs* host custom content using Facebook Markup Language (FBML), and are purely informational. *Custom applications tabs* offer interactivity through media players, forms, quizzes, and games.

Facebook's downsizing of tab widths to 520 pixels made a lot of Page admins nervous, but it still leaves plenty of space to get your message across. Hire a designer or devote in-house resources to developing a few custom Facebook tabs. At this writing, tabs are created using FBML, but Facebook has indicated it might shift to iframes soon. Either way, you'll need a little bit of coding ability to get your Page up and running, but nothing too strenuous for display tabs.

If you plan to push the limits of Facebook customization, you may need to hire someone to build a custom application that runs your tab. This is different from a user-facing application like a game; this app simply provides additional interactive functionality (Figure 7-2) on the tab.

Although a custom application tab may look cool, it's also a lot more work, especially as Facebook changes guidelines for Pages. If you're just starting out in Facebook marketing, stick to a simpler tab initially and consider a more custom solution as an option for down the road once you see how your Page performs.

Figure 7-3. Your posts are what most Page members will see on a daily basis. Give them some personality and include photos and links, like ideeli does here.

Content

Chapter 8 delves into content optimization and development thoroughly, but the topic bears mentioning here as well. Adding and updating content, both in static tabs and as status updates (Figure 7-3), is one of the easiest ways to customize your Page and help it stand out from the pack.

Think about your brand and your business. Does it have a voice? Maybe it's a serious older sister with lots of wise information to impart. Or it could be the wise-cracking sidekick who's always ready with a laugh. Your brand has a tone—a personality—and Facebook is a great place to put that personality to use.

Content is the most malleable piece of a Facebook Page, so you should really make it count. No matter what you are offering on your Page or the tone you want it to take, content customization is key. Find someone who can write well, and not just in lengthy emails and web pages. It takes a special finesse to make a Facebook update interesting, informative, and noticeable in just 50 words or less.

If you've invested in a few general or all-purpose Facebook tabs with room for static content, you can swap out this text and keep your Page fresh without going to the trouble of a full redesign. This will help you customize your tabs and your Page whenever you need to, even if you don't have a full suite of design resources at your fingertips.

Figure 7-4. T.J. Maxx asks Page members to submit their best fashion finds for community voting on Friday. The winner gets featured on the Page, and T.J. Maxx gets a lot of Page interaction.

Branded Patterns and Days

Ideally, you should be posting new content every day on your Page. Status updates are the easiest way to customize and brand your Page. Page members may see them in their newsfeeds or by clicking to visit your actual Page. Each post is a simple, quick way to customize your Page through content.

To bring even more personality to your Page, establish patterns and themes for each day. These over-arching topics allow for flexibility in specific content, while also setting expectations for Page members. It gives them something to look forward to, without giving the entire post away. It will also help them very quickly recognize your posts in their newsfeeds.

You may have seen the user-generated incarnation of this on Twitter with Follow Friday. Many brands have caught on and found great success with the idea on their Facebook Pages (Figure 7-4). Themes can be very overt and consumer facing or more subtle. For example, Fan Friday might highlight an active Page member, while Trivia Tuesday offers fun facts about your brand or industry. You could also try using the theme to guide your content creation. Perhaps Thursday is always the day you give out tips, and Wednesday is for contests. Of course, you don't need to name every promotion as part of Win It Wednesday, and the actual terms and prizes can change. Either way, themes can make developing content much easier and help your Page members choose their favorite days to check your Page.

Figure 7-5. Britney Spears often posts sneak peeks of photos and other media or news first on her Facebook Page.

Exclusive Stuff

You want people to visit your Facebook Page and, ultimately, to visit your website or physical location to purchase your product or service. Unless they're already customers, however, you can't jump in with the hard sell. You need to convince Facebook users to click Like for your Page and then to keep coming back.

Customizing your Page design and content will draw in new visitors, but offering exclusive content (Figure 7-5) will keep them coming back. This is also one of the best ways to stand apart from your competitors, who either can't or won't offer what you do.

Think about what your current customers like. Discounts and secret sales are an easy opportunity for retail Pages, but don't be afraid to think outside the box. Could you give away a special gift to Facebook Page members only? Or offer an off-menu entree they need a secret password to order at your restaurant?

It may sound a little cheesy, but people love to feel special. Exclusivity feeds that feeling and is also a very simple way to customize your Page. Your exclusive deal could change every week or rotate once every few months. Hide it on a custom tab that requires liking to view, and then promote it sporadically through status updates. Most importantly, make sure it speaks to your brand and your Page and offers something no one else can.

Figure 7-6. The New York Times *uses Involver to power a simple yet effective custom tab on its Facebook Page.*

Custom Tabs

Facebook has tried very hard to stay away from the overly customizable options that MySpace offers, but it does allow you to create your own custom tabs. Tabs are currently restricted to 520 pixels wide and cannot contain autoplay content; any interactive functionality must be click-to-engage. Although you are constrained to customizing just a few tabs, you can do quite a bit in that limited area.

If you don't have much coding experience or the resources to hire someone who does, start with a basic tab with a few static images and text. Many free applications provide the basic shell of a tab and enable you to customize within it. Static FBML is the most popular of these, but as mentioned previously Facebook has indicated that it might move toward iframes in the future, so keep that in mind.

Other apps help you create a tab by repurposing existing content. Social RSS is great for pulling in a blog or other RSS channel. The app creates a tab that requires you to enter only a little intro text, a headline, and an RSS feed. Involver, a paid service, also offers a suite of Facebook tab tools that require little to no coding ability (Figure 7-6).

Of course, if you want a fully customized tab, you can build your own application to run the tabs on your Page and have total control over the content display and functionality. This may need to be outsourced, as it requires design and development knowledge.

Figure 7-7. Starbucks created a simple member benefits application that lets you earn rewards at its stores, without having to leave Facebook to sign up on its website.

User Applications

Building an application to fully customize your Page tabs is great—for you. But you can also build a more functional and engaging tab that users will enjoy (Figure 7-7). Creating an application that is fun but relevant to your business can be challenging, but once you have an idea, it can be a great way to market your company on Facebook.

Applications designed for users need to be fun. Often, they are downright silly. Many people use Facebook to kill time, so games and trivia apps are popular. Look at FarmVille, Mafia Wars, or Brain Buddies for inspiration on what you could add to your tabs. Photos are also a big part of Facebook, so applications that allow you to design or decorate photos are usually a hit. Apps like Funny Photo Widget and Picture Frame display albums in cool, unique ways. They also get a lot of traction because people enjoy posting photos to their Walls and newsfeeds, promoting the app for free.

At the heart of it all, Facebook is about people's unique likes and interests, as represented by their Profiles. Applications that capitalize on the often narcissistic tendencies of frequent Facebook users, and create an experience tailored to them, work well. Discovery Channel's Shark Week app made a mini-memorial out of information pulled from a user's Profile, as did a CSI crime scene application.

Whether it's photos, games, or personal experiences, all these apps have one thing in common: they are made for the users, not the brands. That makes them fun to use and quick to spread, which in turn helps the brand.

Figure 7-8. *Facebook's own Page about Pages demonstrates how to customize your content without a lot of fuss.*

Summary

Some say that Facebook's rules for users are too rigid, in particular those for brands managing Pages. While the site does impose some restrictions, Facebook actually offers marketers a wealth of possible opportunities for customization and interaction with fans (Figure 7-8). You may not always have the freedom you desire, but Facebook's decisions are based on careful scrutiny of how users navigate and interact with the site and will help you reach your goals.

You don't have to compete with all of the big brands, just know that they are there. Take cues from what they do and find ways to make those things work for you. Keep on top of the latest trends and updates on the site, and never stop listening to your Page members. They are the most valuable asset you have and will let you know how and where you can better customize your Page to meet their needs.

CHAPTER 8

Developing a Facebook Content Strategy

Given the restrictions Facebook places on Page design, content is the easiest—and often most effective—way to differentiate yourself from competitors. Facebook's power lies in its huge number of users, but this also creates a high volume of posts. To reach these potential customers or brand enthusiasts, your content must stand apart from the rest. Because content is a core piece of a successful Facebook marketing campaign, this chapter explores ways you can create and optimize it for Page members, while at the same time improving your placement in both Facebook and natural web searches.

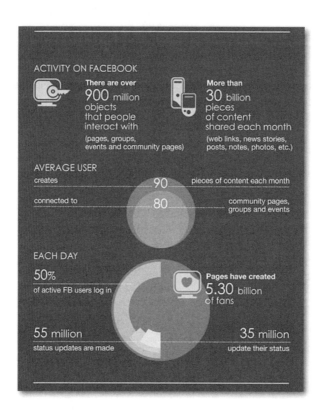

Figure 8-1. There are 900 million people, places, and things that a user can interact with on Facebook. More than 30 billion pieces of content are shared across the site each month. (Graphic by The Blog Herald.)

Competing with Other Content on Facebook

The average Facebook user has 130 friends and is connected to 80 community Pages, Groups, and Events. Yet this is only a fraction of the 900 million people, places, and things that he could interact with on Facebook (Figure 8-1). Considering the more than 30 billion pieces of content being shared across the site *each month*, you can understand clearly why content is a key factor in your Facebook marketing strategy. Obviously, there's a lot that the average user is seeing on a daily basis. But this average user also creates about 90 pieces of content every month—posting links to news stories or blog posts, writing notes, uploading to photo albums, creating Events, writing on friends' Walls, and more.

Since Facebook imposes so many design restrictions, content is the best way to market yourself to potential Page members (and future customers), as well as to keep current Page members and customers engaged and entertained. On the other hand, you must also combat the fatigue many users feel at seeing a never-ending stream of their friends' lunch orders, random thoughts, and recent likes.

Figure 8-2. A typical newsfeed is cluttered with content from Facebook Pages, friends, and applications. A content strategy can help bring order to your posts.

Develop a Content Strategy

A well-thought-out content strategy is the only way to approach Facebook marketing and not drive yourself (and Page members) crazy. It's tempting to just post whatever strikes you that day, but this can quickly become overwhelming, especially when you are competing for attention in a crowded newsfeed (Figure 8-2). A content strategy will help you refine your goals for Facebook. These goals will drive the frequency of posts, as well as their topics or types of content.

Establish Goals

What do you want to do on Facebook? Are you trying to engage people who currently prefer and use your brand? To attract new Page members who already use your service but don't know you're on Facebook? To sell your product or generate leads? Chances are that you said yes to all of these, but they are four different goals that work very differently on Facebook than elsewhere on the Web. Facebook is a *social* network, and while some people will be receptive to sales pitches, the majority are there to talk to friends and connect with brands they really, truly love. To be one of those brands, you need to follow the unofficial Facebook rules of etiquette. That means posting quality information with a frequency and style that matches Facebook: fast and fun. You can tell people about the things you sell, but you've got to strike a balance between interesting or exclusive information and sales links.

Figure 8-3. The top 10 Facebook Pages average just 1.7 posts a day. The most popular Page, Zynga's Texas Hold'em Poker, often posts five times a day.

Determine Frequency

Most Facebook users expect a Page to post new content at least once a day (Figure 8-3). Some prefer a higher volume of posts; others cite this as a reason for unliking a Page. You can't please everyone, but the upside to posting frequently is that more people will catch it in their newsfeeds.

Think about time differences and behavior patterns when posting. If you always post first thing in the morning, many people will miss it as they're on their way to work. They may not even be awake, especially if you are on the East Coast and have Page members several hours behind you. You don't want to simply repost things over and over, however, because at some point, people will go to your actual Page and see a Wall of repeat posts. Vary your language and the way you handle a subject.

The top 10 most popular Facebook Pages post an average of 1.7 updates per day. Of course, they also have an average of over 15 million Page members already. If you are working to attract new Page members, you should probably be posting more frequently, at least in the beginning, in order to quickly populate your Page with great content that will attract return visitors and help you move up in search rankings.

Consider posting once a day at the bare minimum, and aim to post three to five times a day if you have the content and resources to support it.

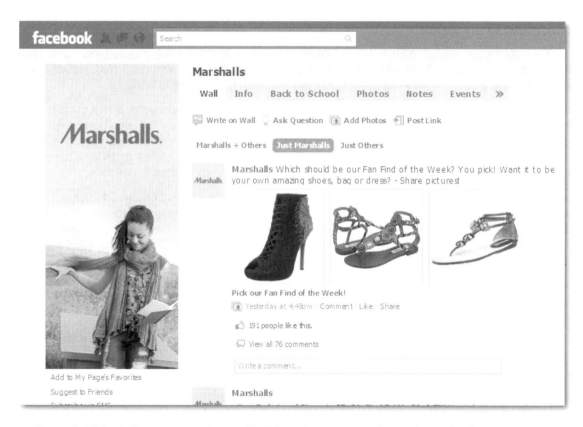

Figure 8-4. Marshalls sets expectations and builds excitement around recurring Friday fan promotions.

Set Patterns and Common Topics

Even if you post only once a day, that's a lot of extra content you need to create each week. Without a sound strategy, the task of creating and posting new content daily can become pretty daunting. What do you want to talk about every day? More importantly, what will people want to listen to and interact with?

Keep writer's block at bay by creating daily features and standard topics for each day of the week (Figure 8-4). This way, when you attempt to write a Monday post, you know the general theme it should follow. A narrow focus actually makes it much easier to write plenty of fresh content and meet your goals.

Having set patterns for content will also keep your Page members engaged as they learn their favorite days for information. You might designate Monday as the day to provide insider information or exclusive Facebook content, such as new store openings, upcoming menu changes, or future product launches. Tuesday might be a day to do more general tips related to your industry, and Wednesday might be contests and giveaways. The actual content always changes, but the topic stays the same. Using a pattern keeps you organized and jump-starts the content creation process, while also conditioning Page members to check back on their favorite days, thereby increasing their likelihood of sharing your content.

DATE	Day of Week	FACEBOOK	TWITTER	MESSAGE TOPIC
8/23	MON	We know our stores are the place to be, but have you tagged yourself at a spot on Facebook Places or Foursquare? Check us out, and check yourself in next time you've got a shoe craving. http://foursquare.com/search?q =shoes	Location, location, location. Everyone's atwitter (aFoursquare?) about checkins. Start working on your mayorship now: http://bit.ly/bGdW 4h	Partner Message or Promotion
8/24	TUES	What's in a name? If you're a high heel, it's a whole lotta lift. Help us out with some "M" names for these Manolos, and make 'em good. 'Cause Martha's just not gonna cut it for these babies.	What's in a name? If you're a Manola stiletto, it's a whole lotta lift. Help us name 'em on Facebook. http://facebook.co m/shoez	Name Game
8/25	WED	Were you a superstar in school? You know, the kid with his hand raised and homework done. Put that studious spirit to good use and share your best shopping tips here. Think of it as Retail101. But instead of a gold star, we're giving out gift cards. ---------- Repost Best Tips	Superstar in school? Put that studious spirit to good use & tell us your best shopping tips. Think of it as Retail101. With gift cards. ---------------------- RT Best Tips	Contest Contest Winner
8/26	THURS	We're still working on a wave. (Have you ever tried to drive and make a shoe symbol with your hands? On second thought, don't answer that.) But we DO have a handshake. Pass it on to the next friend you see. <link to photo>	When we say welcome to the club, we're not kidding. We've got a handshake and everything. Learn it, love it. <link to photo>	Trivia Trip Reminder
8/27	FRI	Fan promotion (need to see photos to write). ---------- Fan promotion winner (need to see photos to write).	#FF ----------	Fan of the Week Follow Friday

MONDAY: partnerships, promotions, philanthropy
TUESDAY: tips, trivia, bi-weekly Name Game
WEDNESDAY: contests, prizes
THURSDAY: Facebook trip reminder, video/media, regional plug
FRIDAY: Facebook contest winner, weekend reminder

Figure 8-5. A content calendar can help you stay organized and on-topic. This one includes both Facebook and Twitter for cross-post continuity.

Create a Content Calendar

Setting topics and patterns is a lot easier with the help of a *content calendar* that allows you to clearly see the dates and days of the week (Figure 8-5). Similar to an editorial calendar but ideal for social media posts, a content calendar is the best way to stay organized and meet your goals. You can develop one exclusively for Facebook or incorporate other sites (like Twitter) to keep the various networks in sync.

A content calendar can be as simple or as complex as you make it. At its very core, it is merely a place to create content ahead of time and map it to days, posting frequency, and topics. Calendars will keep you on track even on the busiest days. Yes, you can write content ahead of time and release it when you are ready. Really. A certain amount of social media actually can be planned or timed. If your goal is to post once a day or more, it is essential to map your posts in a content calendar ahead of time. Of course, be ready to add or move content to react to questions or current events. Still, you should always have at least one good post ready to go.

A calendar also enables you to keep a record of the posts you've made in the past, preventing repetition. With such an archive, you can even track traffic and interaction patterns against content.

ideeli | Facebook
Welcome to the official Facebook Page about **ideeli**. Join Facebook to start connecting with **ideeli**.
www.facebook.com/ideeli - Cached - Similar

ideeli Coupon Codes - all coupons, discounts and promo codes for ... ☆
Average discount of $44.75 with these **ideeli** coupon codes and promo codes. Get the best **ideeli**.com coupon at RetailMeNot.com.
www.retailmenot.com/view/ideeli.com - Similar

ideeli's Brand Director Explains What It's Like to Be One of the ... ☆
Jul 9, 2010 ... Tamara Rosenthal, executive director of brand marketing at New York-based flash sales site **ideeli**, has worked everywhere from Lacoste to ...
fashionista.com/.../ideelis-brand-director-explains-what-its-like-to-be-one-of-the-first-fashion-people-to-embrace-the-internet/ - Cached

Online Sample Sale Site **Ideeli** Raises A Whopping $20 Million
Dec 7, 2009 ... Today, online shopping site **Ideeli**, which was founded in 2007, ... Prior to this round of funding, **Ideeli** raised $3.8 million from Kodiak ...
techcrunch.com/.../online-sample-sale-site-ideeli-raises-a-whopping-20-million/ - Cached - Similar

Results from people in your social circle for **ideeli** - BETA - My social circle - My social content
ideeli | wit & whimsy

WIT & Whimsy - connected via twitter.com
This year, **ideeli** has partnered with Style Coalition to create the Fashion 2.0 Social Media Awards and they want to hear from you! ...
witwhimsy.com/?tag=ideeli
More results from WIT & Whimsy »

Online Private Sample Sales, Rue La La, Gilt Groupe, **Ideeli**, Haute ...
Shoestring Magazine - connected via twitter.com
After France's original private sale site, Vente Privee, became a word-of-mouth sensation in 2002, like most Parisian fashions, ...
www.shoestringmag.com/looks-less/cheap-chic-2008-the-year-private-sale-site

Figure 8-6. Sample sale website ideeli's Facebook Page ranks higher than competing coupon sites in Google results.

Optimizing for Both Facebook and Search Engines

You're probably familiar with *search engine optimization* (SEO) tactics for improving your website's search rankings in Google and other major search engines. But have you thought about how to incorporate social media into your search strategy?

Facebook can be a valuable asset for search results. The volume of content and variety of places to add keyword-rich content can help you attract new Page members on Facebook, while providing more natural search results (Figure 8-6). Facebook is indexed by search engines and also has deals with Google and Bing to display social search results that include posts from your friends.

Facebook's search is not always the greatest at displaying results, but the site's working on it. Counteract its shortcomings with some rockstar SEO to ensure that people looking for your name or service can find you. Misspellings are especially important to account for on Facebook.

In the more general natural-search realm, a well-optimized Facebook Page can help you overtake a competitor by providing a second set of Pages (in addition to your own website) to display on the search results page. This can also be helpful when you're looking to do some reputation management. A Facebook Page can also give you the opportunity to add a few more keywords that didn't work as well on your website.

Figure 8-7. Gilt Groupe keeps it simple with a Page name and URL that match its brand name. The Info Box includes keywords about what Gilt Groupe offers.

The Easiest Places to Put Keywords

The same SEO rules apply for Facebook optimization as for traditional search engines such as Google. Keywords should always be in text fields, and the higher on the Page, the better. Three of the best places are:

Page name

Your Facebook Page name or title is one of the first things both users and search engines see. Create a keyword-dense title, but make sure it's clear who you are and what you do. Your company or brand name is usually the most effective title (Figure 8-7).

URL

You can also choose a vanity URL for your Page, which is another great place to include branded keywords like your company name. Facebook Page URLs are a large part of optimization, as content space is limited.

The Info box

This small, 250-character box located below the Page icon is an underused gold mine for both traffic and SEO purposes. It's one of the first things a current Page member sees when looking at either the Wall or Info tab. The keywords you use in the Info box can go a long way in search. With its prominent placement, the Info box is a great place to optimize a little info about your Page, because it's the highest place in the Page code that allows custom text. You can even put a clickable link in there. You just need to include the *http://* part first.

Figure 8-8. The ASPCA uses a simple yet emotional image on its default landing tab to draw in users. Its tab also has lots of text to ensure it ranks highly and drives maximum traffic.

Using Keywords on Facebook Tabs

The Facebook tab structure creates a helpful hierarchy of information and the ability to add lots of keyword-rich content. Facebook offers several standard tabs for your Page, including the Wall, Info, and Photos or Videos tabs. You can also add your own custom tabs.

Default landing tab

Facebook allows you to choose a specific landing tab for new Page viewers. This is the first tab they see, and its primary goal is to encourage them to click Like for the Page. It is also the first Page crawled by search engines. This default tab can be a custom tab you create, so make sure it contains relevant text that explains to both search engines and Facebook users who you are and what you do.

Info tab

The standard Info tab has fields containing important descriptive data about your Page. It's important to fill out all fields, as they provide an opportunity to include keywords and links for both local searches in the Location field and more general product or service queries in the Company Overview section. The specific fields present will vary by Page category, so choose the category that best fits your needs.

Custom FBML tabs

Facebook Markup Language (FBML) tabs can hold lots of keyword-rich text. You can also include images and links to design the Page and push to more relevant content on your site (Figure 8-8). Adding content tabs to your Page is a great way to drive a ton of traffic in both natural and Facebook search. It also opens up the opportunity to rank for more keywords, including Facebook-specific terms.

Figure 8-9. Victoria's Secret Pink includes videos, photo albums, and links in its status updates. It includes captions for every piece of media uploaded and frequently creates public events.

Other Content

It almost goes without saying, but it's important to continually share interesting content on your Facebook Page and always use all available descriptive fields on each type of content shared. This advice extends past static tabs and into the ever-changing world of status updates and media uploads (Figure 8-9). Facebook allows nearly every piece of content to be indexed by search engines, so use the tabs, tools, and input fields that Facebook provides to your full advantage. Here are a few content-specific tips:

Media

Post photos to multiple albums and include keyword-rich descriptions of the album and each photo. Every event or topic should have its own album for easier searching. Allow Page members to post their own photos and comment on or tag your uploads.

Events

Use the Events feature for both real and virtual events. Always fill out all fields with a full description of the event, and make it open to the public. See Chapter 5 for more information on Events.

Status updates

There is a lot of debate about the extent to which updates help with search engines, but it's clear that they are a big factor in Facebook searches. Take your time when planning content and include keywords; this is the bulk of what Page members will see on a daily basis. You can also add a discussion forum to your Page for even more frequently updated content.

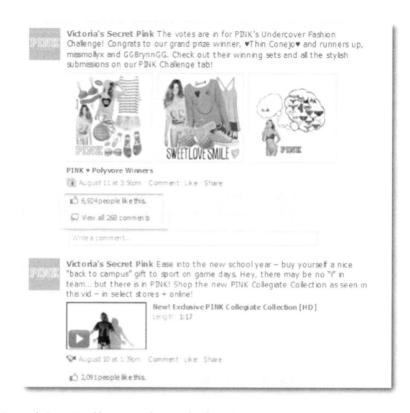

Figure 8-10. Victoria's Secret Pink's strategy has paid off, as the company often receives upward of 5,000 likes or 1,000 comments.

Increased Interactions

User interaction is a crucial yet elusive factor in optimizing your Facebook Page and improving search presence. Facebook views interactions with your Page (likes, comments, and posts) much like a search engine views links pointing to your site. A user interaction is a vote for the content of your Page (Figure 8-10) and helps Facebook rank it higher in its search—and, ultimately, helps your Page rank higher in search engines as well.

Facebook's focus on user behavior and interaction extends to visits, clicks, and Event RSVPs as well. The exact weight or algorithm the site uses to calculate interaction is unclear, but the higher the engagement on your Page, the higher you will rank in Facebook searches and the more prominent your placement in a suggested search.

The predictive search field can most closely be likened to the first page of Google results. Most users never go to the actual Facebook search Page. When a user begins typing in the search box (at the top of every Page), Facebook will suggest friends, Pages, applications, or Events based on her past behavior, the behavior of those she is connected to, and optimization of Pages.

Encourage interaction on your Page by posting frequently and including lots of content that asks users directly to interact. Link participation to prizes: to win, users must vote on photos by liking them or comment on your Wall or posted update. Even without providing an additional incentive, you'll find interaction will spike when you end a post with a question like "What do you think?" Try it—the difference will surprise you.

Figure 8-11. The sheer volume of people and content on Facebook at any given moment necessitates a strong content strategy to break through the clutter. (Graphic by Muhammad Saleem for Mashable.com.)

Summary

The key for Facebook marketing is to keep your Page in the Facebook Newsfeed so that Page members see it, and also to provide content that makes them want to comment, like, or share it. When a user interacts with your content, his friends will see it in their newsfeeds as well, thereby expanding your reach. Optimized content also improves your ranking in both organic search engine results and internal Facebook search results, allowing people actively searching for related terms to find you.

Search engines index social sites like Facebook, so a well-optimized Facebook Page will give you another listing in search results for your company and related industry or service terms. Google and Bing also pull real-time search results from Facebook, so status updates and other timely content could put you on the first page of a search engine results page. Good, keyword-rich content is what fuels both search engine results and Page Member interaction (Figure 8-11). Additionally, interactions on your Page help improve your search rankings, as they demonstrate proof of the Page's quality much like a link would outside in the natural-search world.

CHAPTER 9

Cross-Promoting Content on Facebook

Given its status as the world's largest social network, Facebook is one of the most important and common ways people share content with their friends on the Web. As such, it represents an amazingly large audience for your off-Facebook content. Even when you're creating content outside of Facebook on your own site, you should strive to encourage sharing. Cross-promoting content and driving traffic from your website to your Facebook Page (and vice versa) is an important part of a Facebook marketing strategy. This chapter demonstrates how you can promote your blog and website content so that it gets shared on Facebook.

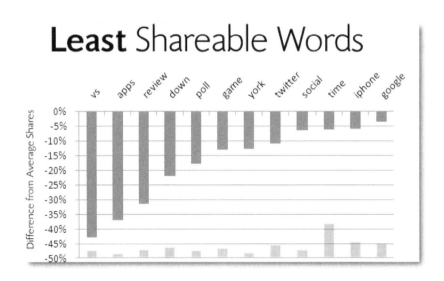

Figure 9-1. Inclusion of these words tends to correlate to an article being shared less than the average on Facebook.

Least Shared Words

If you're used to writing for Twitter, the most important thing to remember is that you're dealing with a much more mainstream audience on Facebook. Topics that entice your typical social media geek won't even raise a Facebook user's eyebrow. Avoid writing about every new iPhone app, Google's every move, or the latest social media fad (Figure 9-1). Of course, if something genuinely newsworthy (and applicable to the nongeek masses) happens in these spaces, then feel free to write about it—just don't do it every day.

While people might be interested in reading reviews of products they're thinking of buying, they're not very likely to share those reviews with their Facebook friends. It also appears that Facebook users aren't big fans of controversial Company-A-versus-Company-B comparisons.

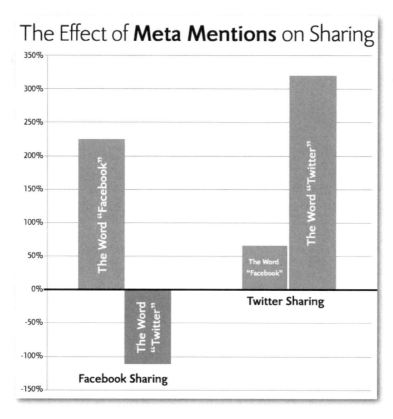

Figure 9-2. Talking about Twitter does not lead to an article being shared on Facebook.

Meta Mentions

The practice of *meta mentions*, in which a user talks about Twitter in a tweet or about Facebook on Facebook itself, produces mixed results. Articles mentioning both Twitter and Facebook did pretty well on Twitter (Figure 9-2). On Facebook, however, articles about Twitter did very poorly, but writing about Facebook itself performed much better. People who are using Facebook are likely to have at least a passing interest in it and probably have some friends who are interested as well. Content about or mentioning Facebook gets shared pretty well across the site itself.

Again, keep in mind that Facebook users are, by and large, not social media geeks, so avoid consistently writing about social media itself. To that end, for content about Facebook to be shared far and wide, it is best to keep it simple and not dive too far into technical comparisons.

Figure 9-3. These words correlate with articles that were shared the most on Facebook.

Most Shared Words

As is the case practically everywhere else on the Web, users aren't that interested in hearing about you on Facebook; they want to read about themselves. When writing for Facebook, tell the reader how your article can help her do something, and use the word "you." Articles with titles like "Top 10 Ways You Can Get Rich" are bound to do well.

The topics and stories you hear mentioned on the nightly news or see on the covers of popular magazines are good things to write about, including political issues and celebrity gossip. Notice the word "says" in Figure 9-3's Most Shareable Words graph: quote people whenever you can, especially people your audience has heard of. Facebook users also appear to appreciate deeper looks at issues. When the words "how" and "why" occur in article titles, those stories do better, on average, on Facebook. TV, radio, and any number of news websites deliver the 15-second sound bite; if you can get behind a story and tell the reader why or how it happened, he might be interested.

Facebook posts can be much longer than a tweet and also allow for formatting. Shorter posts are easier to read and share, but lengthy posts may draw more attention. Experiment with the Notes application and attaching links or images to your Page updates.

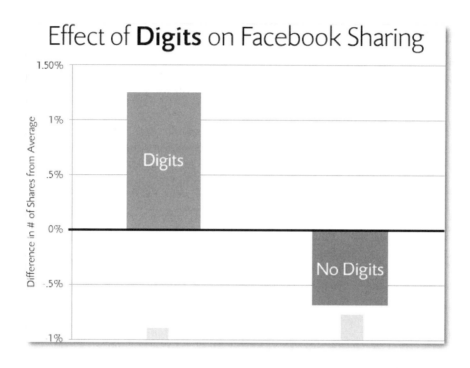

Figure 9-4. Articles with digits in their titles tend to be shared on Facebook more than articles without them.

Digits

When you do make lists, use the digit version of the number. For a variety of reasons, digits work well in almost every context online. Our research has shown that stories that include numbers in their titles tend to be shared more than stories that don't (Figure 9-4). Users aren't so interested in reading generalities; they want specifics, and there's not much more specific than a number. Financial stories should include dollar amounts; environmental disaster stories should include specific figures on, say, the gallons of oil spilled; sports stories should include scores. Any time you can figure out a way to include a relevant digit, do it. In a slightly contradictory finding, we noticed that stories *about* numbers in general tended to be shared slightly less. This metric includes all numbers, digits or not. Mainstream audiences don't want to read many data-heavy and intensive stories, but when they do read these type of stories, they want specifics.

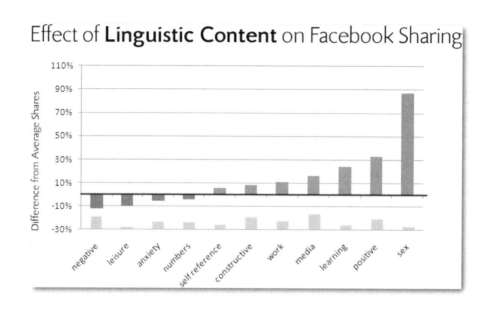

Figure 9-5. Various types of linguistic content affect how articles are shared on Facebook.

Linguistic Content

Using two linguistic analysis algorithms developed by academic researchers—the *Regressive Imagery Dictionary* (RID) and *Linguistic Inquiry and Word Count* (LIWC)—we were able to investigate cognitive and emotional content of links shared on Facebook (Figure 9-5). The most shared type of content isn't very surprising when you remember that Facebook started with (and is still very popular among) college kids. Facebook users like sharing stories about sex. If you're feeling daring, go ahead and try to write something scandalous. For most marketers, however, this isn't the most practical advice.

The Power of Positivity

We were initially somewhat surprised to find that positive stories did much better than negative ones, but after we thought about it a bit, it made sense. There is no lack of negative news stories in the media, and most people aren't going on Facebook to get depressed. They're there to socialize with their friends, and that usually means feeling good, not bad. Try to write positive stories as much as you can, and when you have to cover something negative, try adding an upbeat, hopeful spin.

Try a Teaching Moment

Two other types of content that tended to perform well in our study are constructive and educational content. These are articles that teach readers something, either about the world around them or how to actually accomplish something. Remember that a good way to title an article like this is to specifically state that the article will teach the reader ("you") something.

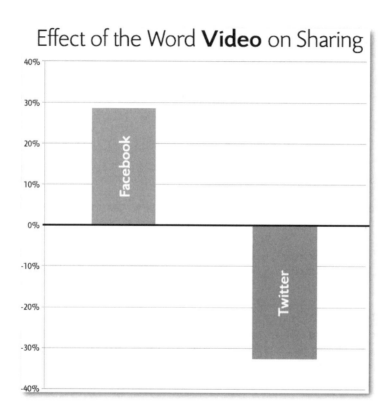

Figure 9-6. Articles that have the word "video" in their titles tend to be shared on Facebook more than articles that don't.

Video

Just like their offline mainstream counterparts, many Facebook users like watching videos. Another bit of research we conducted found that articles that announced they contained a video were shared more than those that didn't (Figure 9-6). In another testament to the differences between the Facebook and Twitter audiences, those same stories tended to get retweeted less. This is likely due in part to the fact that Facebook has a feature that pulls the video content of a posted link and embeds the video (where it can) directly into users' feeds. You can take advantage of this by either producing your own videos and uploading them to YouTube or by simply embedding videos related to your article.

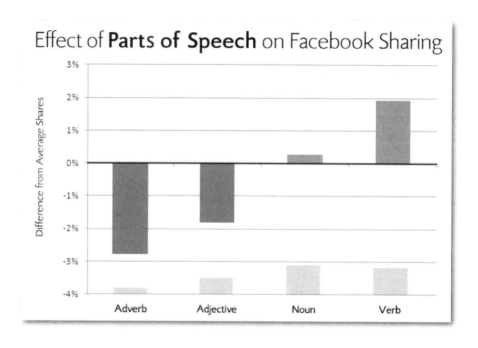

Figure 9-7. Articles that use adverbs and adjectives heavily tend to be shared less on Facebook than articles that don't.

Parts of Speech

One of the best books about writing is a short tome called *The Elements of Style*, but most people know it by its two authors' names: Strunk and White. It contains a series of rules, essays, and exhortations about proper grammar and style, and teaches many great lessons, especially about the importance of direct and terse language. Nowhere are those lessons more valuable than on the Web. Browsing users are bombarded with far more articles than they could ever hope to read, and most of those stories are laden with superlatives and bombastic claims. Not only are we overloaded with information, but we're becoming numb to the most shocking stuff. The adjective and the adverb are the main weapons abused by the spam-headline and tabloid-style blog writers. When we looked at the parts-of-speech content of stories shared on Facebook, we found that modifiers in headlines tend to bode poorly for the performance of an article (Figure 9-7).

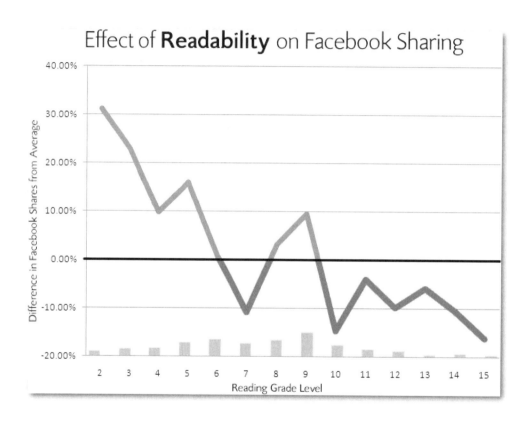

Figure 9-8. Articles that require a high level of education to read tend to be shared less on Facebook than simpler ones.

Readability

Stay away from flowery language. The information you're presenting should be strong enough to shine through a simple and direct headline. Of course, there are exceptions: certain niches online, most notably photography and design, have been successful using adjectives like "stunning" and "amazing," but use these with caution. Reading level scores indicate the grade level needed by a reader to fully understand a piece of text. You're probably familiar with scores like the Flesch-Kincaid reading level embedded in Microsoft Word. In previous research, we found that retweets tended to have comparable (or slightly higher) required reading abilities to understand than tweets that were not retweeted. But when we used readability metrics to look at stories shared on Facebook, we found a very different situation (Figure 9-8).

As the complexity and education level required to read a story increased, the number of times it was shared on Facebook decreased. Once your article is much tougher than grade-school level, you should expect it to be shared far fewer times than it would have been had it been written at a lower level. Make your headlines and articles simple, direct, and easy to read.

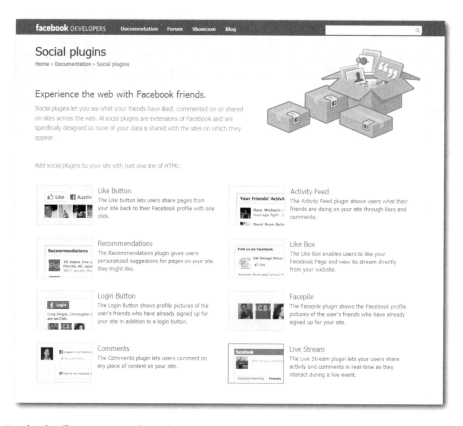

Figure 9-9. Facebook offers a variety of social plug-ins that allow you to integrate social features into your website.

Social Plug-ins

Facebook offers a number of features, called *social plug-ins*, that you can add to your site to integrate your content with Facebook (Figure 9-9). The three most useful are the Share button, the Like button, and the Activity Feed.

The Share Button

The Share button is the oldest of the three features and the most common. It is a piece of JavaScript code that you copy and paste (*http://developers.facebook.com/docs/share*) onto your site to create a button displaying the number of times that Page has been shared on Facebook. This also allows visitors to share it themselves with one click. The button can be shown as a link, but we recommend not using this version. Facebook gives you the option to include the share count on the button or not. Including the count is the best option, as it not only draws more attention to the button, but also adds a form of social proof to your content, prominently displaying how many other people liked your work.

Figure 9-10. *This is the screen you'll see when you're creating a Facebook Share button to include on your site.*

Customizing the Share button

When you add the Share button code, Facebook presents you with options to customize it (Figure 9-10). The Above Button and Inline With Button options for positioning the included counter essentially determine the size and orientation of the button. Selecting to display the count above means that Share will generally be shown as a larger, vertical button, whereas selecting inline makes it much smaller and horizontal. The larger count-above button works best on single content Pages, such as permalink Pages on a blog, while the count-inline style is best on Pages with multiple pieces of content displayed, as on a blog home page. Conveniently, when at least one person has shared your content, the count-above button matches the size and the layout of the popular Twitter buttons, meaning the two can (and should) be displayed together. There is a small issue with the button that causes it to be displayed in a much smaller version when there are no shares yet. If you're displaying both the Tweet and Share buttons together, they may look a little funny when your content is first published, before anyone has liked it. If you are implementing the Share button in a content management system (like a blog), you'll probably want to pass certain values to the button dynamically. You do this by inputting values into the JavaScript code that is pasted into your site.

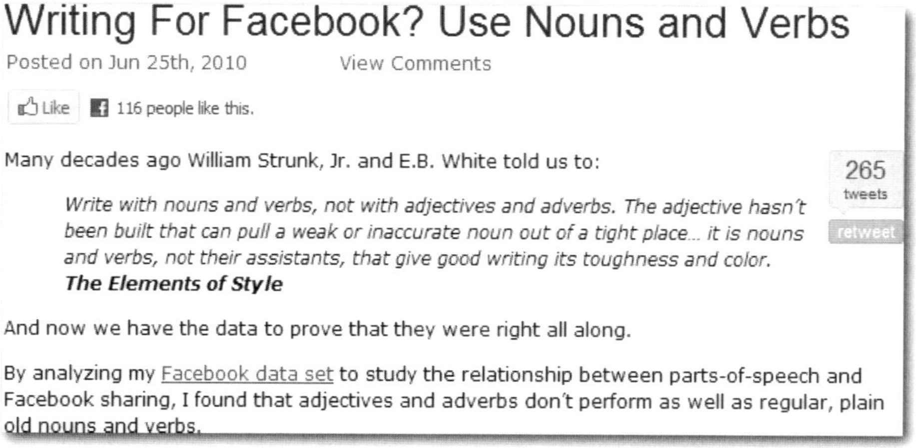

Writing For Facebook? Use Nouns and Verbs

Posted on Jun 25th, 2010   View Comments

👍 Like   ❚ 116 people like this.

Many decades ago William Strunk, Jr. and E.B. White told us to:

> *Write with nouns and verbs, not with adjectives and adverbs. The adjective hasn't been built that can pull a weak or inaccurate noun out of a tight place... it is nouns and verbs, not their assistants, that give good writing its toughness and color.*
> **The Elements of Style**

And now we have the data to prove that they were right all along.

By analyzing my Facebook data set to study the relationship between parts-of-speech and Facebook sharing, I found that adjectives and adverbs don't perform as well as regular, plain old nouns and verbs.

265
tweets

retweet

Figure 9-11. The Facebook Like button is a powerful call to action to entice your visitors to share your content with their friends.

The Like Button

Facebook's Like button is similar in implementation to the Share button, but adds functionality (*http://developers.facebook.com/docs/reference/plugins/like*). Adding the Like button requires you to copy and paste JavaScript code. Once the button is on your page, it shows how many people have liked your content, while also allowing visitors to like it with one click. Unlike Share, this button appears in only a small, horizontal version (Figure 9-11).

The Like button takes the social proof aspect of the Share button to an entirely new level: if a user's friends like your content before she views your Page, the button can show her the names and images of those friends.

Customizing the Like button

When you set up your Like button, Facebook offers you two versions: *standard* and *button count*. The button count version resembles the inline Like button in size and layout and may be used to replace it. The standard version is the most common and recognizable version. Although you have the option to Show Faces or not, you should choose to show them. Facebook also enables you to change the verb displayed on the button: you can select either Like or Recommend from the drop-down menu. In most cases, Like is preferred and the most common, but in certain circumstances (such as a specific product page), you may want to experiment with showing Recommend.

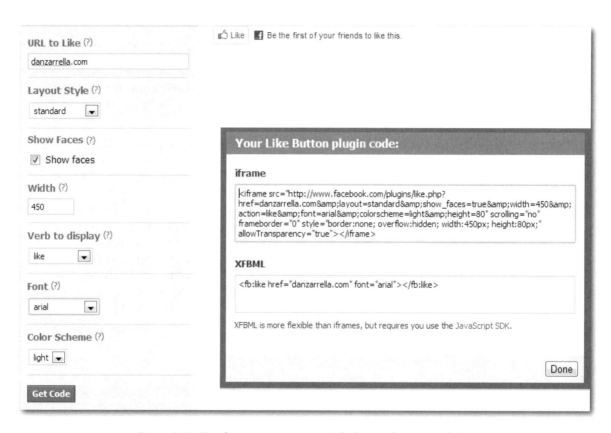

Figure 9-12. Use this screen to create a Like button for your website.

Finally, Facebook asks you to provide a maximum width for the button as well as a color scheme and a font. The width should be determined by how much space you have available in your layout, and the font by the dominant font on your site. We recommend sticking with the default color scheme—light—because it includes the colors and shades most common to Facebook (Figure 9-12). As with the Share button, you may want to pass certain values to the Like button dynamically. To do so, simply input values into the JavaScript code that is pasted into your site.

Like or Share?

The Like button includes many of the benefits of the Share button in that it allows your visitors to post your content to Facebook with a single click, and it shows readers how many people have also liked or shared your content. There are some trade-offs between the two buttons, though. While the Like button has the large advantage of showing visitors exactly which of their friends have liked your content, it is much smaller than the Share button, and therefore, may attract less attention.

Figure 9-13. The Facebook Recommendations box allows your visitors to see content from your site that has recently been shared on Facebook by their friends.

The Activity and Recommendations Feeds

The third type of social plug-in Facebook offers you to cross-promote your content are the feeds: Activity and Recommendations (Figure 9-13). Both are narrow boxes that display content from your site that a visitor may be specifically interested in. The Recommendations feed contains content suggested by Facebook based on overall activity, while the Activity feed shows your readers the content from your domain that their friends have liked. The Activity plug-in includes an option to display Recommendations, so we advise that you use it to get the benefit of both. When you're setting up your Activity feed plug-in, Facebook asks several questions related to the design of the feed box, including font, border color, height, and width. As with the Like button, your choices here are dependent on the space available in your site's design. Stick to the default light color scheme, because it is the most similar to Facebook itself. To install an Activity feed plug-in on your site, copy and paste the JavaScript code provided by Facebook (*http://developers.facebook.com/docs/reference/plugins/activity*). There is really no reason to change values dynamically.

Summary

When you think of Facebook marketing, you probably think first about interacting with users on Facebook.com itself. The truth is that there is a lot of Facebook activity that occurs on external websites, so you should spend some time thinking about how to integrate your content that lives outside of Facebook into the social network itself.

We've done a lot of research to help you learn how to write for Facebook. It's most important to write simply, plainly, and for a mainstream audience. This includes both the topics you choose and the language you use to write about them. Remember, writing for Facebook can be very different than writing for the social media enthusiasts on Twitter.

To better share your content, Facebook offers a range of social plug-ins that enable you to leverage certain features of Facebook from your site. They're simple to integrate and provide great social value to your readers, so take advantage of them.

CHAPTER 10

Facebook Page Management

Managing your Page ensures that you have a finger on the pulse of your consumers, helps attract and keep members, and can assist direct marketing initiatives beyond Facebook. As an extension of your website but offering a lot more user freedom, your Page must be monitored. You need to keep an eye on your Wall, specifically the good (and the bad) reviews from Page members.

Like it or not, what people post on your Page's Wall is a reflection of your brand. If you allow it to be overrun with spam, foul language, or unanswered questions or complaints, your brand will suffer. You need to push out fresh content, sure, but you also need to engage with people on your Page. This chapter teaches you how to keep your Facebook Page full of fresh content and how to keep Page members happy.

Figure 10-1. Exclusive offers, information, or deals entice users to click Like and keep coming back to the Page. Overstock.com's Page offers special coupons just for Facebook Page members.

Exclusive Deals for Fans

One of the best ways to gain Page members is by offering them something—more specifically, something they can't get anywhere else. By providing an exclusive offer, discount, deal, sneak peek, or source of information, you've given them a tangible reason to like your Page and to keep coming back (Figure 10-1).

This tactic is even more effective when combined with a landing tab reveal: a tab view that promises an exclusive offer to new visitors, then changes to reveal that offer once they click Like. This allows you to immediately deliver on your promise and prove your Page to be valuable, all with one click.

Facebook doesn't allow on-site tracking, but an exclusive offer can be a great way to track the success of your Facebook marketing plan as measured by traffic to your site. Create unique links or promo codes for Facebook-only deals. Promote these links or codes exclusively on Facebook, and track redemption or clicks on your site the way you would with any promotion.

These deals don't need to be excessive, or even different from some standard offers you might use to persuade new customers or give out at events. You just need to repackage them for Facebook and make sure they're not too easy to find elsewhere. For example, if you readily send 10% off coupons to new customers, try that tactic here as well.

Figure 10-2. Given that there are over 500 million users and 900 million things to interact with on Facebook, you need to post frequently to keep your page in the Newsfeed and compete with the big brand pages. (Chart courtesy of DBM/Scan and AdvertisingAge.com.)

Frequent Status Updates

As you read in Chapter 8, it's important to post frequent status updates or Wall posts with new information, contests, or deals for your Page members. Many major marketers rely on this tactic to stay ahead of the competition (Figure 10-2). You should, too: aim for a minimum of one post per day and consider a few days with more frequent content.

The trick is to keep users entertained without clogging their newsfeed and annoying them. Make sure each post has a reason (not just "to get one done") and take the extra few minutes to ensure that it is quick, easy to understand, and engaging. Don't forget to spellcheck, and think about what kind of media or links you could include to make the update stand out. Again, a content calendar can help with a lot of this planning.

Remember to account for time differences if your business appeals to people in multiple time zones. Even if you're concentrated in one geographic area, vary your posting times to see what works best. You might miss people if you consistently post right at 9 a.m. every morning.

The most important thing to remember when posting updates is that there are lots of other Pages on Facebook, all competing for a share of space in the Newsfeed. You want to keep your brand appearing in that feed, and you want your content to keep people clicking to your Page or sharing with friends. Give them a reason to keep coming back, and provide content they want.

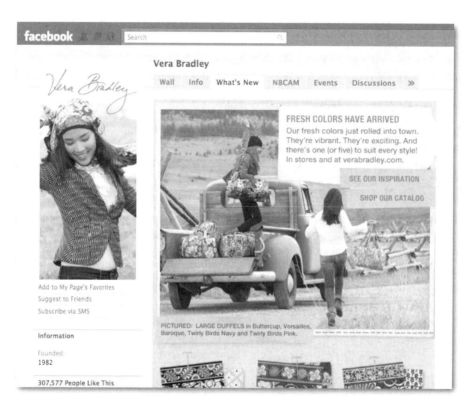

Figure 10-3. Vera Bradley uses several custom tabs and updates them frequently to match the company's ongoing promotions and seasonal styles.

Timely Redesigns

So you're posting status updates at least once a day and keeping a steady stream of content flowing on your Wall and in the Facebook Newsfeed. But what about the rest of your Page? One of the best things about Facebook is how much simpler it can be to update a tab on your Page than a page on your website.

You should think about a Facebook Page refresh at least four times a year. You could, for example, tie these changes to the seasons, as fashions change for the weather and menus reflect in-season produce (Figure 10-3). Even if your business isn't as tied to seasonal changes as some others, you can still take a cue from the changing weather and preferred activities. Or just think of these transitions as gentle reminders to update your Page. If you have a lot going on, you can even update once a month.

Your status updates provide a daily dose of new content, but these are just small snippets of what your Page has to offer. Revamping the look and messaging of your tabs ensures that even your long-term Page members stay loyal, while also persuading new visitors to click Like based on your timely landing tab.

It's a good idea to have one "meet us" type of tab that is fairly consistent in messaging, but with a changing look. The rest of your tabs can rotate in and out to feature contests, promotions, events, and news. Play around with them and see what works.

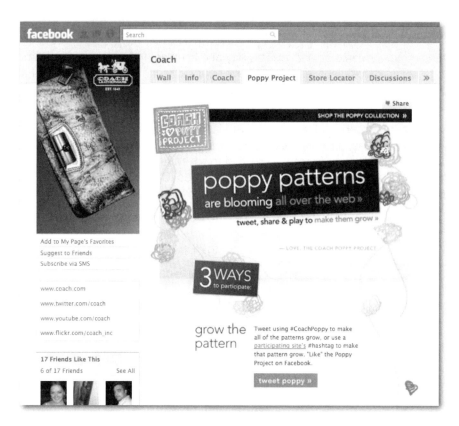

Figure 10-4. Coach created a dedicated promotional tab for its Poppy Project.

Promotions

A promotion is, by nature, a limited-time kind of thing. Whether it's for a Facebook contest, in-store event, or online sale, a promotional tab (Figure 10-4) is designed to be updated fairly frequently. Short-term, one-day promotions (store opening sales, limited-quantity items, or that day's restaurant special) can be covered in a status update or two. Long-term promotions, however, warrant their own tab, unique to that specific promotion. You can also create a catch-all promotions tab and swap out the content as needed.

Unique Promotion Tab

A tab dedicated to a unique promotion is best used for bigger, long-term promotions that run for at least a few weeks. Such a tab typically requires Page members to do something and offers a more sizeable payoff than a quick 10% coupon or free soda.

Design the tab specifically to reflect the promotion and include some sort of functionality to involve members, whether it's a form, link, or interactive game. You should run only one of these at a time, but they can run in conjunction with other short-term promotions. Remember to occasionally plug this promotion with a status update and link to the tab.

General Promotions Tab

A general promotions tab is a great feature if you have limited design capabilities but want to offer some cool stuff to Page members. Invest in one standard promotional-themed tab design with easily interchangeable content slots for the details. This allows you to run different offers at once, or keep members informed of upcoming promotions to look for.

Figure 10-5. HomeGoods keeps a close eye on its page, awarding contest winners promptly and providing updates and advice on how to vote in its contest.

Monitoring

The goal of your Facebook Page is to attract and engage fans of your brand, building a community for Page members. While increasing interaction by encouraging questions and comments is a solid strategy and an integral part of your Facebook marketing plan, it also generates a lot of user content and commentary that must be monitored (Figure 10-5).

Many services offer automated Facebook monitoring (a quick Google search for "social media monitoring" provides a host of free and paid tools), but there really is no substitute for human interaction. That means actual on-Page eyes from someone on your team who can take the pulse of the Page and respond to questions, complaints, and compliments.

You do not need to be watching your Page all day, but you should check in at least once. If you're posting frequently, see what's going on then. Keep in mind that most action might be clustered right after you post, so check back shortly after that, too. Of course, if you're running a Facebook promotion, you'll need to be picking winners and answering questions.

You can't spend all your time responding to generic "love your Page" comments, but pick and choose the posts where you can provide helpful commentary. Make your presence known, but don't be overbearing. Encourage the community aspect, and let it do most of the talking.

Figure 10-6. As home to a popular brand with 1,659,232 members, Target's Facebook Page is a hotbed for spam comments and brand backlash.

Moderation

Monitoring your Page is only half the battle, however, and when it comes to time, more like only 25%. You must also moderate your Page and make judgment calls on which types of posts should be deleted, responded to, or left alone (Figure 10-6).

How you determine what stays and what goes is up to you. Some Page admins remove all negative feedback; others leave it and respond to the criticism as best they can. A good rule to follow is to leave legitimate comments, both positive and negative, for all to see. Respond to both kinds of posts, either with a "thanks for the kind word" message or an appropriate response to questions and complaints.

Yes, some people like to use social media just to complain. But it's usually pretty easy to pick out the ones who just want to cause trouble from the ones who want your help resolving an issue. If they ask for a solution, try to give it to them, but don't feel tied to responding exclusively through Facebook. A simple message like "we hear you and will get back to you with how we can resolve this" can go a long way. Post this on the Wall to show you heard their cries, then message them privately to get contact information and fix the problem behind the scenes.

Beware of spam posters as well. You want to keep your Wall open for comments related to your brand and industry, but keep an eye out for people posting links that push their own agenda and remove them before they get in the way of your Page members' experience.

Figure 10-7. Boutique fashion retailer Gilt Groupe does a great job of responding to member questions on merchandise and upcoming sales.

Responding

So you've deleted the obviously spammy or bogus comments, but what about the real customer service issues? If something went wrong, it's time to fix it.

You can answer general questions fairly quickly, and they might benefit from both a comment on the user's existing post as well as a general status update (Figure 10-7). You can call out the person who asked the question to show you're listening. Something like "Thanks for the reminder, Jason! Yes, it's summer, and we've extended our hours. Stop by anytime from 9 a.m. to 10 p.m. Hope to see you soon."

If the question or complaint is more personal, you may have to do some research and probably want to follow up offline. Diplomatic honesty is usually going to be your best bet here. Read the complaint, then take a step back. If you're not familiar with the situation, talk to someone who is. You want to get all the facts before you present a solution. In the meantime, post a message letting the poster know you're working on it. Then send her a private message to get her preferred contact info and resolve the issue over phone or email.

Don't forget to say thanks for praise and comment on relevant articles or stories posted on the Page! Doing so can help foster a sense of community. Take a moment to respond to happier comments, too.

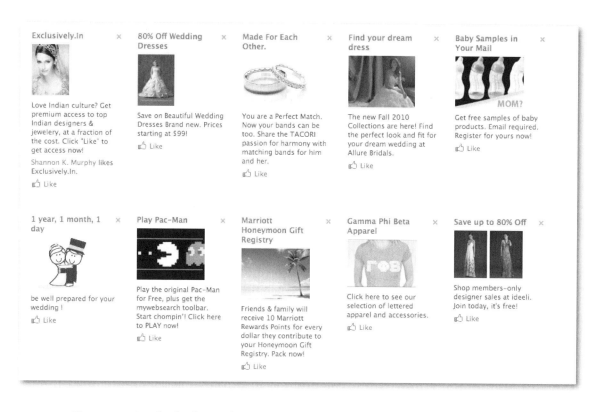

Figure 10-8. Facebook ads are often tied to specific landing pages, either on or off Facebook. When your landing page changes, so should your ad.

Advertising

Your Facebook ads should be updated at least four times a year, just like your tabs. Facebook advertising (Figure 10-8) is perhaps one of the most targeted advertising vehicles online, and you can play with millions of possible parameters. Experiment to find out what works, and don't be afraid to switch things up or run some tests.

Swapping out ads is even easier than updating a tab, as you have limited space and design capabilities. But don't let that fool you. You should never change an ad just because it's time. Make sure there is a strategy for every change and that the advertising unit is geared toward helping you reach a marketing goal.

These goals could fluctuate throughout the year, from gaining Page members to increasing interaction to eventually driving traffic to your website. Facebook ads that drive off-site should be clear about the end location. You might even create a specific landing Page acknowledging that people came from Facebook. This helps ease their transition, while also aiding with your tracking and allowing you to easily deliver on Facebook-exclusive deals.

Facebook ads that direct users to your Facebook Page should always have a corresponding landing tab. So when you change up your tabs, it's probably time to update your ads, too. Remember, keep your content fresh. This applies to anything related to your Facebook Page, even ads.

Figure 10-9. Victoria's Secret Pink is always ahead of the curve in Facebook marketing. Look to it for examples on content updates, redesigns, and member responses.

Summary

Remember, your Facebook Page is a representation of your brand or business, just like your website, email or print marketing materials, and physical locations. It's great to recognize that Facebook is an important place to be from both a user and search perspective, but just showing up is not enough. You have to use Facebook effectively. That means logging in, posting content, and responding to what's happening on your Page (Figure 10-9).

Listen to your members. Thank them, respond, and follow up offline to resolve issues. Automated Page monitoring can help fill in the gaps, but you need a real person to read through comments and assess which ones require responses. Only a human can truly detect the tone of a post, and only someone familiar with your brand or business will know how to respond.

This is the nature of Facebook, and if you must post your own content less frequently in order to respond to people, so be it. A Page that ignores its members and just shouts its own messages all day is not using Facebook correctly.

Remember, sometimes responding doesn't mean posting a comment. It could mean listening and making a change. If everyone posts that they hate a certain menu item, don't just say, "Thanks for the suggestion." Change it. Where else can you get such brutally honest feedback? Use it to your advantage.

CHAPTER 11

Advertising on Facebook

Facebook has a powerful advertising platform known as Facebook Ads. Low click-through rates, sophisticated targeting options, and easy integration with applications and Pages make it an interesting tool for marketers. Facebook Ads can be especially helpful for kick-starting your Facebook presence, and some of the most powerful social targeting features become useful when you have a large number of Page members or users. This chapter introduces the platform and walks you through creating and launching an ad.

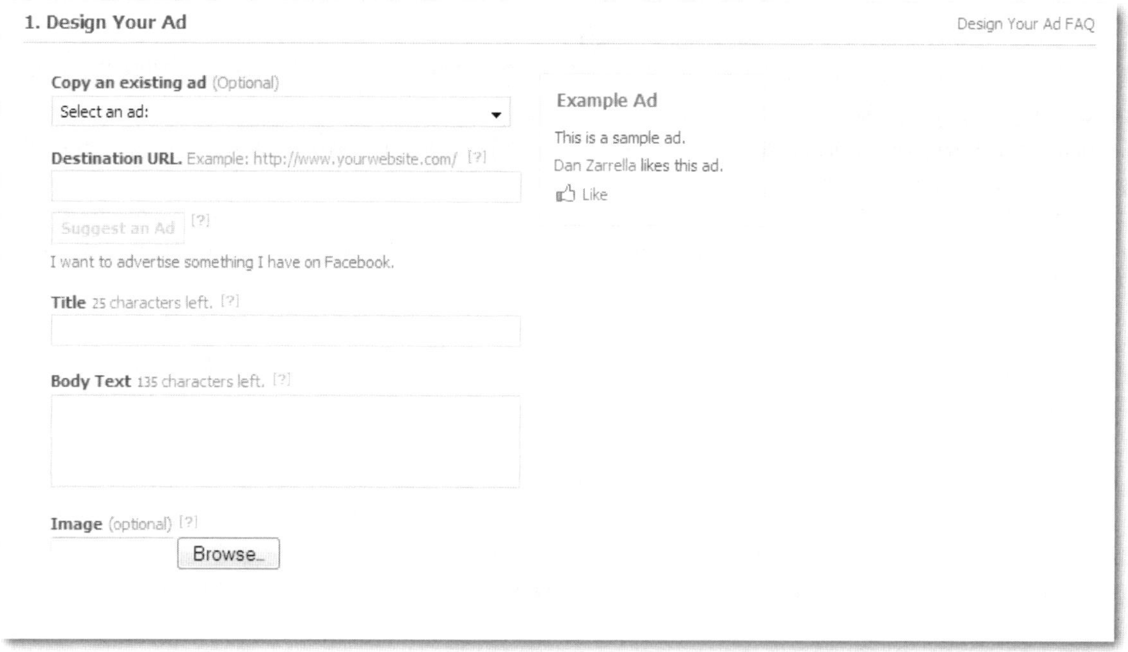

1. Design Your Ad

Design Your Ad FAQ

Copy an existing ad (Optional)

Select an ad: ▼

Destination URL. Example: http://www.yourwebsite.com/ [?]

Suggest an Ad [?]

I want to advertise something I have on Facebook.

Title 25 characters left. [?]

Body Text 135 characters left. [?]

Image (optional) [?]

Browse...

Example Ad

This is a sample ad.

Dan Zarrella likes this ad.

👍 Like

Figure 11-1. Use this form to create your Facebook ad.

Where to Send Users

Remember why people use Facebook: it's not to view your ads and then go to your website. They're on Facebook to use Facebook itself. Use the Facebook Ads platform to send people to applications or Pages on Facebook itself, not external websites. Make sure to provide a seamless user experience as well. To create an ad that sends traffic to your Page or application, click the "I want to advertise something I have on Facebook" link (found at *http://www.facebook.com/ads/create/*) and select the destination from the drop-down menu (Figure 11-1).

If you really want to send people to another site, you can enter a destination URL. Remember to include tracking tokens so you can accurately track traffic from your ads. Chapter 12 goes into more detail on this.

Creative Content Design

When you're creating your Facebook ads, remember that you're talking to a mainstream audience that is interested in socializing with friends. The creative elements—images and copy—that make up your ads should reflect this as well.

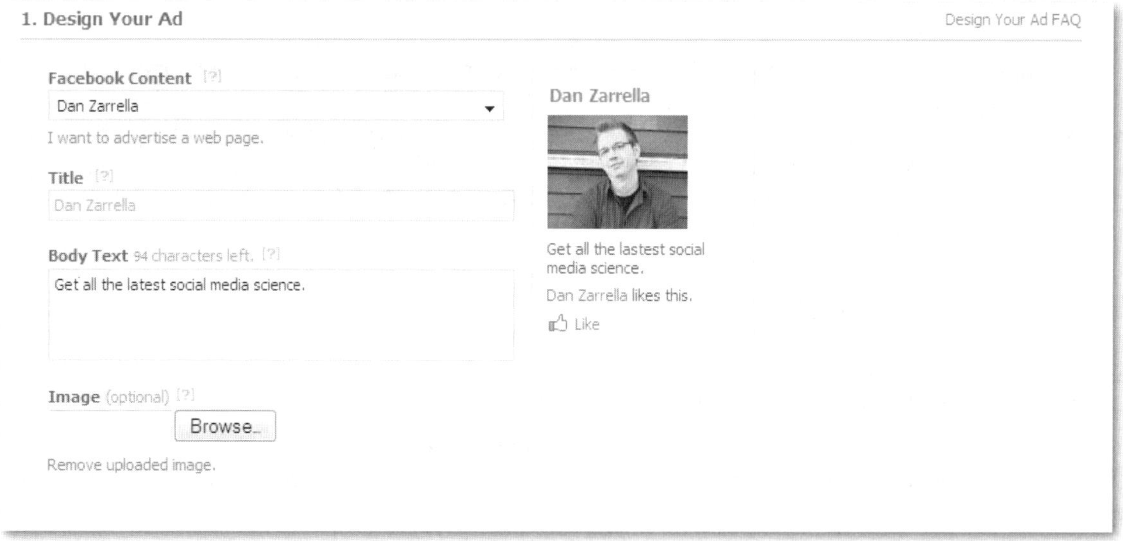
1. Design Your Ad
Design Your Ad FAQ
Facebook Content [?]
Dan Zarrella
I want to advertise a web page.
Title [?]
Dan Zarrella
Body Text 94 characters left. [?]
Get all the latest social media science.
Image (optional) [?]
Browse...
Remove uploaded image.
Dan Zarrella
Get all the lastest social media science.
Dan Zarrella likes this.
Like

Figure 11-2. Selecting a good image is key to creating an attractive and attention-grabbing Facebook ad.

Images

Facebook ads are composed of a title limited to 25 characters, a body of 135 or fewer characters, and an image under 110 pixels wide and 80 tall. The most important part is the image; it will draw the user's eye first (Figure 11-2).

There are big differences between images for Facebook ads and those for print and web ads. Professional-looking ads aren't best on the social network. Facebook users don't click on a lot of ads while there; they're not trying to be marketed to and they won't be impressed by high production values.

Facebook users are looking at user-generated content, so your ads should reflect that. Stay away from highly polished stock photography. They're also looking at mostly pictures of people, so you'll do well to use images of real people in your ads. Remember the visual context surrounding your ad. Facebook is mostly white and blue, so experiment with photographs in contrasting warm colors. Sometimes, louder tactics such as three-dimensional-looking buttons, bright red borders, and lens flares can work, but use these sparingly and test frequently.

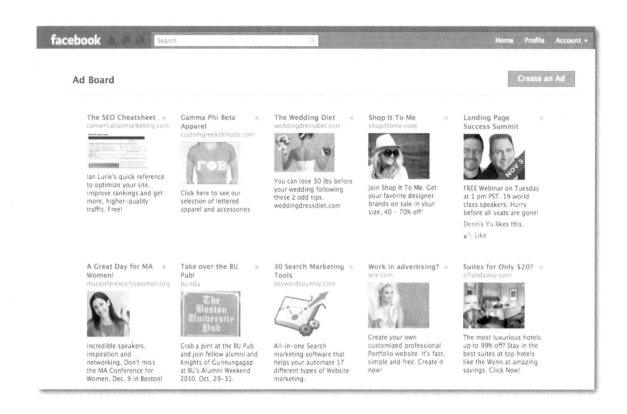

Figure 11-3. As you create your ad, Facebook shows you a preview of what it will look like when it's displayed on the site.

Copy

The written part of your ad will be a short title and a body. If you've ever written *pay-per-click* (PPC) ads, you should feel fairly at home with the microcopy format. These character-limited ads need to get to the point quickly in a very small space, while making good use of keywords for targeting. However, they also need to sound natural. Committee-crafted or jargony sales pitches will be alien on Facebook. Speak simply and plainly with very little flowery language. Don't use too many adjectives or adverbs, and don't use SAT vocabulary words.

You are writing for a mainstream audience. Be as direct and specific as possible. Include very clear calls to action that tell the user exactly what you want him to do, and indicate that the action can be completed quickly and easily. Use words like "now" and "today" to tell users that they can get started right away (Figure 11-3). If users can expect to get results from your ad, use specific digits to let them know. If you're going to charge them a price, tell them the exact amount.

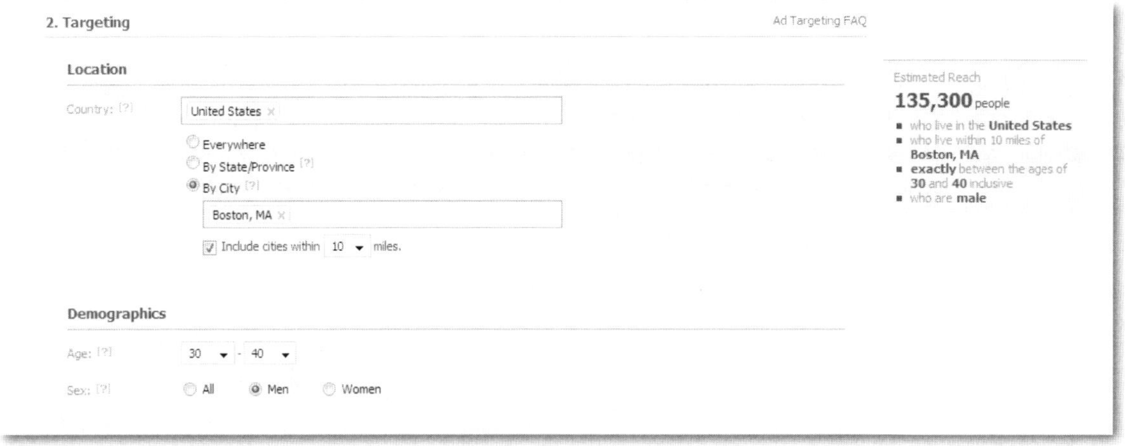

Figure 11-4. The Facebook Ads platform allows you to target users by geography and demographic information.

Targeting

The most powerful feature of Facebook Ads is the incredible targeting it allows you to do. Because users provide mounds of data about themselves, you can identify very tight groups of people to advertise to. Take advantage of this as much as possible; your campaigns should include lots of highly targeted ads being shown to small subsets of people. Facebook will guide you through different target criteria as you create your campaign.

Location

Geography is the first dimension Facebook allows you to target with (Figure 11-4). Facebook Ads are very useful for local businesses—even global or national brands that have some local connections. Select the smallest local area you possibly can. Create specific ads for different cities and talk to readers in the local parlance. The more you know about the place you're advertising to, the better.

Demographics

Facebook will also allow you to choose age and gender specifications. Again, try writing separate ads to appeal to people of different sexes and ages. Men and women use Facebook differently, as do people in various age groups. While researching your exact audience, you'll uncover specific preferences, but you can start with hints from the ads you see on television and from the covers of magazines aimed at different groups. Also keep in mind that older users may be more conscious of privacy issues, so don't ask them for a lot of personal information.

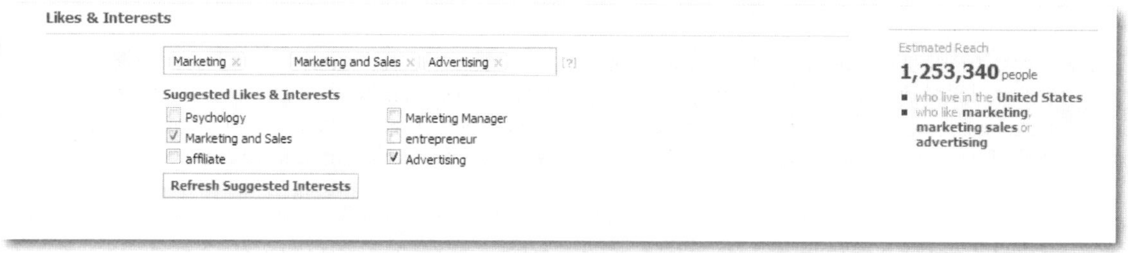

Likes & Interests

| Marketing × | Marketing and Sales × | Advertising × | | [?] |

Suggested Likes & Interests

- ☐ Psychology
- ☑ Marketing and Sales
- ☐ affiliate

- ☐ Marketing Manager
- ☐ entrepreneur
- ☑ Advertising

Refresh Suggested Interests

Estimated Reach
1,253,340 people

- who live in the **United States**
- who like **marketing, marketing sales** or **advertising**

Figure 11-5. As you continue targeting your Facebook ad, including likes and interests, Facebook shows you the estimated number of users your ad will reach.

Likes and Interests

When a user fills out his Profile, he adds information about his interests, activities, favorite books, movies, television shows, and more (Figure 11-5). Using the Facebook Ads platform, you can specify keywords to target users who have used the same words in their Profiles. Search engine marketing will provide a great list of keywords to start with, but you might have to go a step further for your Facebook ads. Think about interests that may not be directly related to your business but indicate that a user may be interested in your brand.

Relationship and Interested In

If you're offering a dating or relationships-based product or service, use the Relationship and Interested In fields liberally. In fact, depending on what you're selling, you may be required by Facebook's Terms of Service to use them. For most businesses, however, these fields will be of little use.

Workplaces

If you're doing business-to-business (B2B) marketing, especially to large companies, the Workplaces field can be a gold mine. Target ads to specific enterprises to which you'd like to sell your product or services.

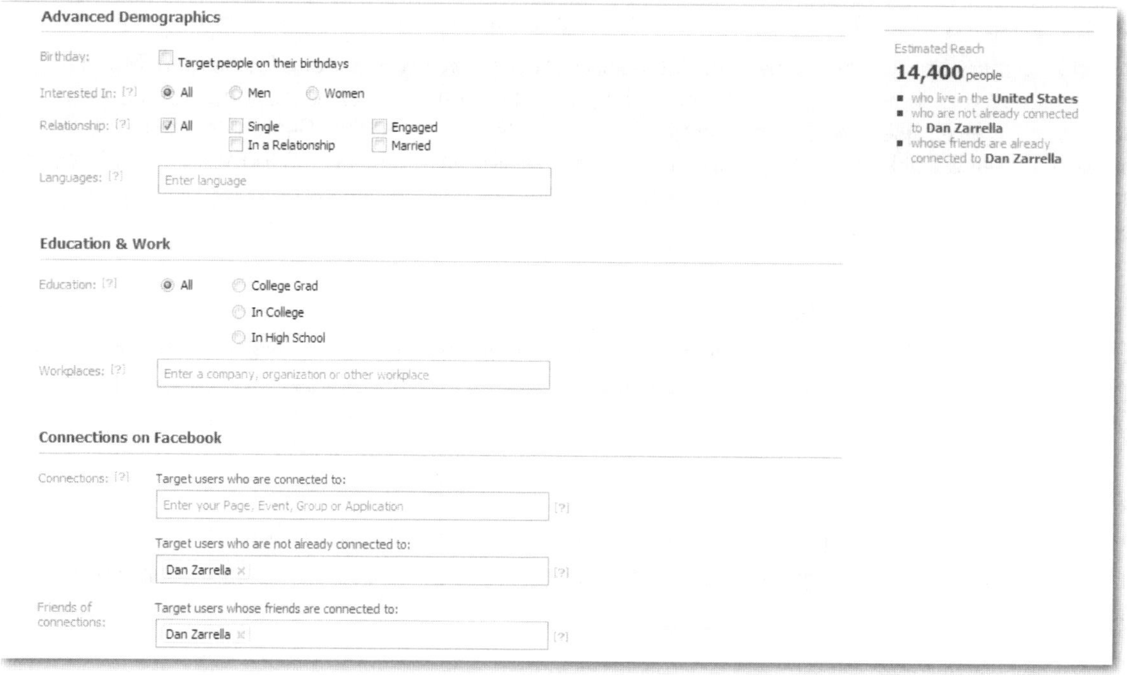

Advanced Demographics

Birthday: ☐ Target people on their birthdays

Interested In: [?]   ◉ All   ○ Men   ○ Women

Relationship: [?]   ☑ All   ☐ Single   ☐ Engaged
                                       ☐ In a Relationship   ☐ Married

Languages: [?]   Enter language

Education & Work

Education: [?]   ◉ All   ○ College Grad
                                       ○ In College
                                       ○ In High School

Workplaces: [?]   Enter a company, organization or other workplace

Connections on Facebook

Connections: [?]   Target users who are connected to:

                              Enter your Page, Event, Group or Application   [?]

                              Target users who are not already connected to:

                              Dan Zarrella ×   [?]

Friends of   Target users whose friends are connected to:
connections:
                              Dan Zarrella ×   [?]

Estimated Reach

14,400 people

- who live in the **United States**
- who are not already connected to **Dan Zarrella**
- whose friends are already connected to **Dan Zarrella**

Figure 11-6. Facebook Ads includes advanced targeting options such as social connections.

Connections and Friends of Connections

If your application or Page already has a sizable fan base, you can use the Connected To field to nurture users who are already familiar with your brand, persuading them to become even more engaged or moving them along the sales process (Figure 11-6). Ask users if they'd like to talk to a live representative or offer them special fan-only discounts. You can use the Not Connected To field to show ads only to users who aren't connected to your presence on Facebook. It can be useful to show less direct-response, introductory ads to these users. Using the Friends of Connections field (one of our favorites), you can target people who are friends with Page members or application users. Not only does this allow you to target social groups who are likely to be interested in your brand (if their friend is, they're likely to be as well), but when a user sees an ad for a Page or application a friend is connected to, it shows a "John Doe likes this" line underneath. This is an incredibly powerful example of social proof: a user is much more likely to pay attention to an ad if someone she trusts is essentially recommending it.

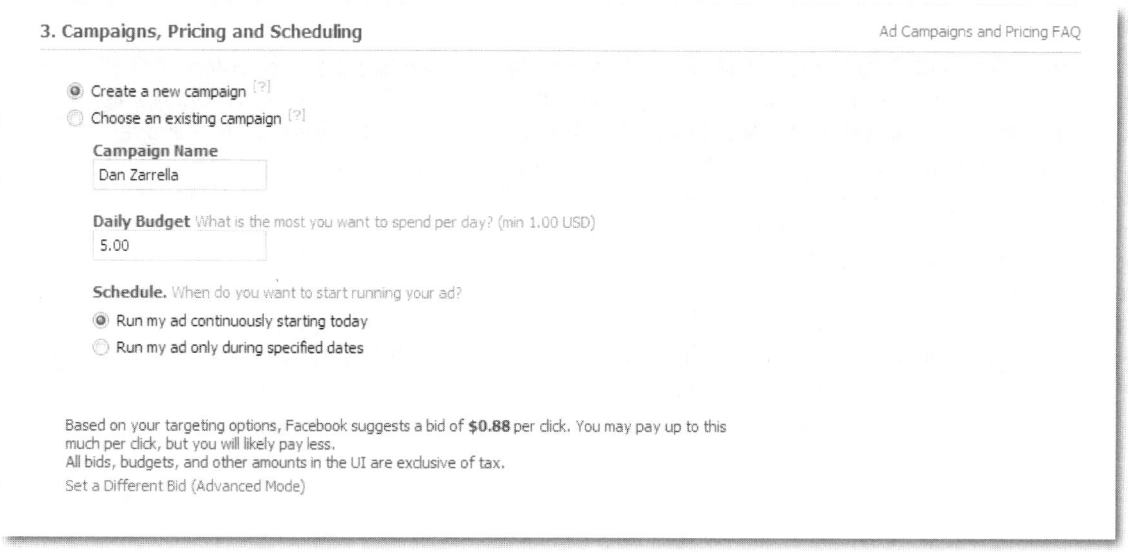

3. Campaigns, Pricing and Scheduling

Ad Campaigns and Pricing FAQ

○ Create a new campaign [?]
○ Choose an existing campaign [?]

Campaign Name

Dan Zarrella

Daily Budget What is the most you want to spend per day? (min 1.00 USD)

5.00

Schedule. When do you want to start running your ad?

◉ Run my ad continuously starting today
○ Run my ad only during specified dates

Based on your targeting options, Facebook suggests a bid of **$0.88** per click. You may pay up to this much per click, but you will likely pay less.
All bids, budgets, and other amounts in the UI are exclusive of tax.
Set a Different Bid (Advanced Mode)

Figure 11-7. After you create and target your ad, you need to put it into a campaign and set a budget.

Budget

The first time you create an ad, Facebook Ads requires you to create a new campaign to put your ad into (Figure 11-7) as well as a daily budget. The daily budget is the dollar amount you're willing to pay every day to run your ads; once you hit this limit, Facebook stops running your ads for the rest of the day.

When you're starting out, assume you're going to spend this budget every day and select an amount you're comfortable spending. It's a good idea to start low until you get a good idea of the amount of return you will see from your ads. Check out Chapter 12 to learn how to measure the value you're getting.

Figure 11-8. When setting your ad budget, you can also opt to pay per click.

Bidding

The bottom of Facebook Ads' creation Page presents you with two options for ad pricing:

- Pay for Clicks (CPC)
- Pay for Impressions (CPM)

Because the click-through rate on Facebook ads tends to be very low, you'll probably want to use a CPC model, meaning you pay only when someone actually clicks your ad. Under this model, you'll get thousands of impressions without paying for thousands of clicks, and it is generally the cheapest way to pay. By default, Facebook suggests a bidding model and price in what it calls Simple Mode (Figure 11-8). For most purposes, this suggestion works fine. Let your ad run for a few days or weeks. If you're hitting your budget every day, experiment with lowering your bid gradually. You may be able to squeeze a few more clicks out of your investment this way.

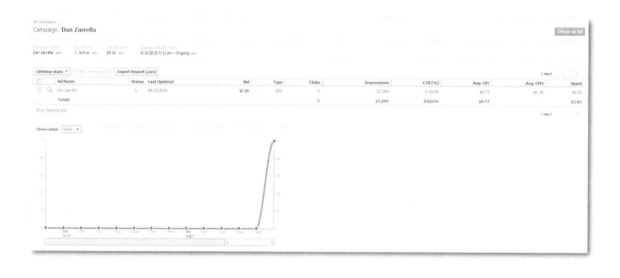

Figure 11-9. Once your ad is running, Facebook shows you some basic information about impressions, clicks, and cost.

Ad Stats

Clicking Submit sends your ad to Facebook for an editorial review. The ad must be approved before it starts to run. The decision is typically made pretty quickly. Once your ad starts to run, Facebook provides some simple statistics about it, which you can view on the campaign management Page (*http:// www.facebook.com/ads/manage/campaigns.php*). The page displays graphs of impressions and clicks over time as well as bidding and budgeting information (Figure 11-9). This data is great for keeping an eye on how much you're spending and for spotting opportunities to lower your bids. If you're sending traffic to a Page or application, check out the insights Facebook gives you about the people using those. If you're sending people to a different site, look into your own analytics packages. Again, be sure to read Chapter 12 to learn more about analytics and return on your investment.

Summary

Ads can help you jump-start your Facebook marketing campaigns. Take advantage of their highly targeted nature and be sure to measure and monitor their performance.

Because viewers aren't looking for ads when they're on Facebook, you'll need to be creative when you're designing the images and writing the copy for your ads to attract attention. Many current Facebook ad campaigns are riddled with typos and bad grammar, so take care when crafting copy. Plenty of brands look for an easy solution and get sloppy with their promotions. Don't be one of them. Invest a little extra time to create a good ad and an efficient bidding plan—you'll reach your goals faster in the end.

CHAPTER 12

Analytics and ROI

As with any marketing efforts, closely tracking the success of Facebook marketing is extremely important—not only to justify your investment but also to improve your future work. Facebook itself includes a robust analytics platform known as *Insights*, which allows you to gather information about your Pages, applications, and ads. You should also be aware of how your Facebook marketing campaigns are affecting the performance of your properties outside of Facebook. This chapter teaches you how to do both.

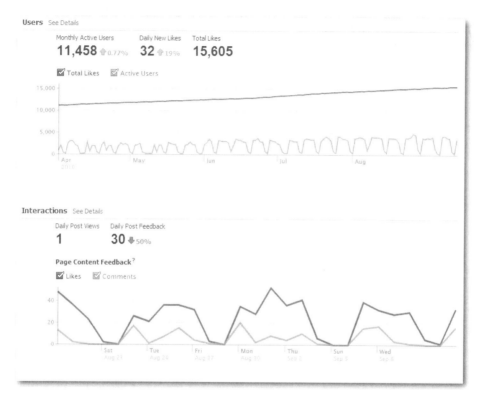

Figure 12-1. Facebook's Insights platform allows you to see basic or detailed information about the performance of your Pages.

Insights for Page

Facebook's native analytics platform, Insights, allows you to access detailed information about fans of your brand that is otherwise very difficult or expensive to obtain. Navigate to your Page, and you'll see a link to the Insights Page in the left sidebar. Basic user statistics available through Insights include daily and monthly active users, daily new likes, and total likes over time (Figure 12-1). These metrics are fairly shallow, but they're a great way to establish and monitor trends, especially your rate of daily new likes and daily active users. Generally speaking, as long as these benchmarks are all increasing, you're headed in the right direction. The basic interactions data will look much more variable than your user statistics. This graph shows you the likes and comments on your Page on a daily basis. The amount of content posted to your site (as well as the quality of that content) will probably vary. Your goal with this data is to maintain a baseline of activity on most days. Detailed user data provided by Page Insights includes a breakdown of your daily active users, allowing you to see what percentage of them simply visited your Page. You can then compare this with more engaged users who liked or commented on a post, or posted their own message to your Wall. For most Pages, the majority of users will be merely visitors, but you should encourage your users to perform more engaged actions.

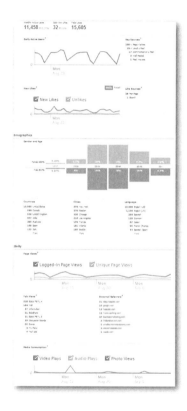

Figure 12-2. Facebook Insights gives you extensive demographic, geographic, and activity-based data about users who have liked your Pages.

Likes and Unlikes

The detailed user data allows you to track not only the number of likes received by your Page over time, but also the number of unlikes that occurred. The number of unlikes will typically be very small compared to likes, but a large spike could indicate a problem you should investigate.

Demographic Data

On the detailed user Insights Page, you can also dig into very detailed demographics data about your users, including age, gender, location, and languages spoken (Figure 12-2). This kind of information can be useful for informing your Facebook marketing efforts as well as your non-Facebook campaigns.

Activity and Traffic

The Activity tab of the detailed user data Page shows you where the activity on your Page occurred and the origin of the traffic. You'll see a list of tabs alongside the number of views each received, as well as a list of external sites that drove traffic to your Facebook Page. Below those two tables, Insights shows you data on the media consumption that occurred on your site, including video and audio plays and photo views.

Figure 12-3. Through Insights, you can see activity on your page on a per-post basis.

Feedback on Facebook Posts

On the detailed interactions Page, Facebook shows you daily story feedback information with a graph displaying likes, comments, and unsubscribes over time (Figure 12-3). Again, you want the first two metrics increasing, and a large spike in unsubscribes should set off some alarms. Below the daily story feedback graph, there is a list of stories posted to your Page and the number of impressions each story received as well as a feedback percentage. The feedback percentage is the portion of users who interacted with a story somehow—larger is better. This chart is very useful for refining the content you post to your Page. Notice which subjects get the most views and feedback, and pay attention to the days and hours that seem to be the most popular. The Page activity graph shows the amount of activity undertaken by users on your Page, including discussion, Wall and video posts, reviews, and mentions. This graph shows the activity day to day, so it will be very bumpy.

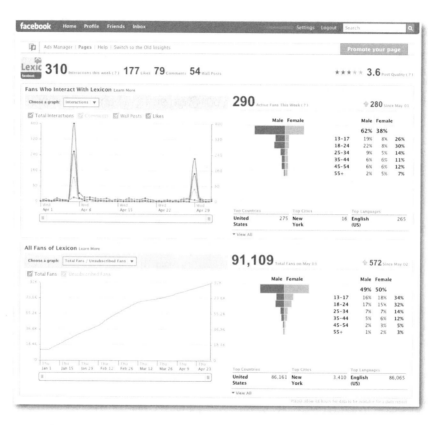

Figure 12-4. Facebook Insights for applications gives you information about users of your application.

Insights for Applications

Much like the native analytics for Pages, Facebook allows marketers to view detailed statistics about the usage of their applications (Figure 12-4).

The Users section of application Insights includes information on monthly and daily active users (*MAUs* and *DAUs*). MAUs and DAUs are the most important and visible metrics about an application's popularity. They indicate the number of users who have interacted with an application in a given month or day. Most applications will have many more users who allow an application access to their Profile (effectively "installing" the application) than those who regularly use it. MAUs and DAUs are the easiest way to monitor how engaged your application's users are. Facebook shows the same demographics information about applications as it does about Profiles, including age, gender, location, and languages. It also shows simple data about the number of views to an application's canvas Page, as well as the number of users who gave the application permission to access their Profile. The goal for any marketer is to see these numbers trend upward over time.

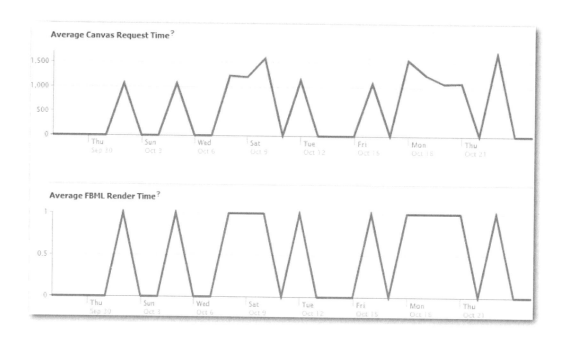

Figure 12-5. Facebook Insights also gives you information about the performance of your application from a technical point of view.

Posting Application Content to Walls

Applications often allow users to post content to their own Profiles, and Facebook shows information about this content in the Sharing section of application Insights. Facebook displays the number of stories, status updates, and photos posted through the application as well as the amount of feedback (likes and comments) this content received. You can also monitor the number of times this content was hidden. Sharing content is an important viral mechanism for an application, so this data is a good way to monitor how social your application is and how well it is doing in generating interest from your users' friends. The third and fourth sections of the application Insights interface include performance and diagnostics information (Figure 12-5). For marketers, the key points here are to keep an eye on the request and rendering time your application takes to display content to users. Work with your developers to ensure that this trends downward over time as your application gets faster, and be aware if there is a major upturn in these times.

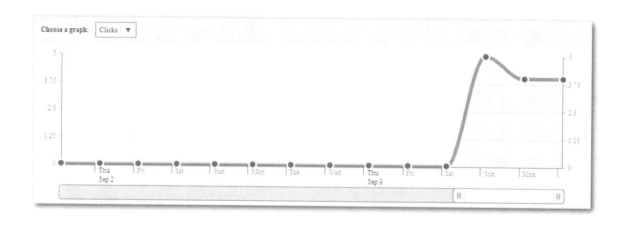

Figure 12-6. Facebook's Ads platform gives you basic information about the number of clicks your ads have received over time.

Facebook Ads Analytics

The Facebook Ads platform shows you some basic information about clicks, impressions, and click-through rates over time. With it, you can also create reports about ad performance as well as responder demographics and Profile information. The campaigns Page of the Facebook Ads interface provides basic statistics about your campaigns, including the number of clicks, impressions, and cost (Figure 12-6). You'll also find a graph that displays impressions, clicks, and click-through rate over time. This data is useful only for very high level, at-a-glance monitoring of your ads.

Advertising Performance Report

The reports section of the Ads interface allows you to generate more detailed reports about your ads. The first of these reports is Advertising Performance, which includes information about clicks, impressions, conversions, and actions. The last metric, actions, is the most important and useful. If you're advertising a Facebook-based Page or Event, the Actions column shows the number of times viewers of the ad liked your Page or sent a yes or maybe RSVP to your Event through the ad itself.

View Advertising Report

Export Report (.csv) | Generate Another Report | Schedule this Report

Report Type	Summarize By	Time Summary	Date Range
Responder Demographics	Campaign	Monthly	07/01/2010 - 09/12/2010

Date	Campaign Name	Demographic	Bucket 1	Bucket 2	% of Impressions
Aug 2010	Dan Zarrella	country	US		100.000%
Aug 2010	Dan Zarrella	gender_age	F	18-24	89.815%
Aug 2010	Dan Zarrella	gender_age	F	25-34	6.736%
Aug 2010	Dan Zarrella	gender_age	F	35-44	1.671%
Aug 2010	Dan Zarrella	gender_age	F	45-54	0.438%
Aug 2010	Dan Zarrella	gender_age	F	55-64	0.291%
Aug 2010	Dan Zarrella	gender_age	F	65-100	1.049%
Aug 2010	Dan Zarrella	region	us	Massachusetts	98.669%
Aug 2010	Dan Zarrella	region	us	Washington	1.331%
Sep 2010	My Ads	country	US		100.000%
Sep 2010	My Ads	gender_age	F	18-24	95.792%
Sep 2010	My Ads	gender_age	F	25-34	4.208%
Sep 2010	My Ads	region	us	Alabama	0.264%
Sep 2010	My Ads	region	us	Arizona	0.490%
Sep 2010	My Ads	region	us	California	9.450%
Sep 2010	My Ads	region	us	Connecticut	0.468%
Sep 2010	My Ads	region	us	Florida	5.669%
Sep 2010	My Ads	region	us	Georgia	3.465%
Sep 2010	My Ads	region	us	Illinois	3.487%
Sep 2010	My Ads	region	us	Indiana	1.252%
Sep 2010	My Ads	region	us	Kansas	0.259%
Sep 2010	My Ads	region	us	Louisiana	0.608%
Sep 2010	My Ads	region	us	Maryland	1.348%
Sep 2010	My Ads	region	us	Massachusetts	35.863%
Sep 2010	My Ads	region	us	Michigan	3.025%
Sep 2010	My Ads	region	us	Mississippi	0.248%
Sep 2010	My Ads	region	us	Missouri	1.531%
Sep 2010	My Ads	region	us	New Jersey	2.333%
Sep 2010	My Ads	region	us	New York	9.419%
Sep 2010	My Ads	region	us	North Carolina	3.853%
Sep 2010	My Ads	region	us	Ohio	1.522%
Sep 2010	My Ads	region	us	Pennsylvania	4.356%
Sep 2010	My Ads	region	us	South Carolina	0.673%
Sep 2010	My Ads	region	us	Tennessee	0.945%
Sep 2010	My Ads	region	us	Texas	4.364%
Sep 2010	My Ads	region	us	Virginia	2.640%
Sep 2010	My Ads	region	us	Washington	1.400%
Sep 2010	My Ads	region	us	Wisconsin	1.067%

Figure 12-7. You should select specific metrics to measure, as they affect your marketing campaigns. These are your key performance indicators (KPI).

Responder Demographics Report

The second type of report you can generate from this interface is Responder Demographics (Figure 12-7). This report shows you the gender, location, and age breakdown of the users who clicked on your ad. This information can be used in conjunction with demographics information from your Page or application to refine the targeting of your ads so they're only shown to the most important and effective users.

The third report type is Responder Profiles, which allows you to see information from the Profiles of users who have clicked on your ads. This includes interests, books, music, and TV shows. You can use this information to refine (or broaden) the targeting of your ads. If you notice that many users who have clicked your ad have listed a common interest, you can create an ad that speaks directly to that niche.

Figure 12-8. Using a third-party analytics system, you can track how many visitors your Facebook efforts have sent to your site and how well they performed.

Goals and KPI

The ultimate point of analytics is to measure how effective your marketing efforts are in obtaining certain goals. Before you launch any campaign, you should clearly understand what your goals are: are you trying to drive sales of a product? Are you striving to generate leads for a service? Are you interested in sending traffic to your site to monetize through ad clicks? Or are you trying to increase awareness and buzz around your brand? Goals of the first three varieties are generally easier to report and are closely tied to profit, making them powerful metrics to justify investments of time and money in Facebook marketing.

Once you've decided on your ultimate goals, you need to identify *key performance indicators* (KPI) to measure (Figure 12-8). These are metrics that indicate the effectiveness of your efforts in achieving your goals. If you're trying to drive sales, then the most important KPI would be sales attributed directly to Facebook marketing; if your goal is leads, then your main KPI would likewise be leads attributed to Facebook traffic. In addition to these direct KPIs, it is advisable to define proxy or intermediate metrics to watch. Typically, these are the potential actions of a user who is likely to complete a goal. Because many of these profit-driving goals take place off of Facebook, it can be useful to measure the engagement levels of the traffic Facebook is sending to your site. Engagement metrics include numbers like average-time-on-site and Page-views-per-visit.

Figure 12-9. The most important metrics of any campaign are those that actually affect your bottom line.

Tracking

Most commercial websites already have an analytics package installed to monitor user activity. Google Analytics is a common, useful, and free example. If you have goals already set up in your analytics system (as you should for any type of marketing, not just Facebook), you'll likely be able to measure the performance of traffic coming from Facebook.com in your referrers reports (Figure 12-9). Watch the amount of traffic Facebook is sending your site as well as time-on-site and page-views-per-visit metrics as intermediate KPIs. Ultimately, you'll want to pay the most attention to the number of direct goal completions (sales, leads, and so on) resulting from Facebook.com traffic. Analytics packages like Google Analytics also allow you to use tracking parameters to refine the level of information you see about Facebook traffic. If you're using a Facebook ad to send traffic to your site, add these parameters to the end of the target URL to see the performance of traffic coming to your site from specific ads. Each analytics package handles tracking parameters differently, so the best place to learn about them is directly from your package provider (for example, there are a number of books and websites that can teach you how to use parameters with Google Analytics).

Summary

As a marketer on Facebook, you're there to do business and make money, not just make friends. It is vital that you track the performance of your efforts and how they relate to your company's bottom line.

Facebook allows you to easily analyze the activity on your Pages, applications, and Facebook ads with its Insights system. Use Insights for both high-level and detailed analytics.

If you're integrating your Facebook marketing efforts with your external website (as you should be), you can also use your non-Facebook analytics system to track the effectiveness of the new traffic you're driving from the social network.

Acknowledgments

Many thanks to our moms, and to Barbara and Jenn, our little sisters. Also to BJ, Gramma and Grumpa, Nana and Pa, Terri and Joe Devito, and the rest of our family. This book was a labor of love, and you each helped in your own way.

From Dan: Thanks to the whole Hubspot team, but especially: David Gallant, Brian Whalley, Kyle James, Kyle Paice, Kipp Bodnar, Yoav Shapiro, Mike Volpe, Jeanne Hopkins, Brian Halligan, and Dharmesh Shah. Also to Mari Smith, Guy Kawasaki, Brett Tabke, and Nancy Duarte for their professional wisdom.

From Alison: Thanks to my friends, on Facebook and in life: Lindsay White, Kristin Burnham, Ashley Cannon, Laura Seddon, Erica Pritchard, Debbie Keene, Stephanie Piotrowski, Jacky Fontanella, Marla Napurano, Treasa Law, Courtney Livingston, Judiann McNiff, Dylcia Morell, David Abend, Tina Morelli, Steve Bonda, Tom Moran, Andre Docarmo, and Fabricio Blasius. To Brett Tabke and the whole Webmaster World crew, for letting me talk about Facebook to anyone who will listen. And to all my fellow Zipsters who help me do what I love every day, especially Mandy Donovan Drake, Bob Burns, Stephanie Shore, and Rob Weisberg.

Index

Colophon

The cover, heading, and text font is Helvetica Neue. The caption font is Minion Pro.

About the Authors

Dan Zarrella, social media scientist at HubSpot, has written extensively about the science of viral marketing, memetics, and social media for a variety of popular industry blogs. His work has been featured in news outlets including CNN International, the *Wall Street Journal*, the *New York Times*, and more.

Alison Zarrella is an interactive copywriter and social media consultant. She has worked on Facebook marketing and content strategy with a variety of clients, ranging from small local businesses to global brands. She has written for industry blogs such as Mashable and has been featured as a social media and Facebook expert in multiple media outlets and guest lectures.

Get even more for your money.

Join the O'Reilly Community, and register the O'Reilly books you own. It's free, and you'll get:

- 40% upgrade offer on O'Reilly books
- Membership discounts on books and events
- Free lifetime updates to electronic formats of books
- Multiple ebook formats, DRM FREE
- Participation in the O'Reilly community
- Newsletters
- Account management
- 100% Satisfaction Guarantee

Signing up is easy:

1. **Go to: oreilly.com/go/register**
2. **Create an O'Reilly login.**
3. **Provide your address.**
4. **Register your books.**

Note: English-language books only

To order books online:
oreilly.com/order_new

For questions about products or an order:
orders@oreilly.com

To sign up to get topic-specific email announcements and/or news about upcoming books, conferences, special offers, and new technologies:
elists@oreilly.com

For technical questions about book content:
booktech@oreilly.com

To submit new book proposals to our editors:
proposals@oreilly.com

Many O'Reilly books are available in PDF and several ebook formats. For more information:
oreilly.com/ebooks

O'REILLY®

Spreading the knowledge of innovators   oreilly.com

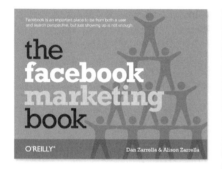